AFRICAN AMERICANS OF DURHAM & ORANGE COUNTIES

AFRICAN AMERICANS OF DURHAM & ORANGE COUNTIES

AN ORAL HISTORY

JEAN BOLDUC

FOREWORD BY ANTHONY WILSON

THE History PRESS

Published by The History Press
Charleston, SC
www.historypress.net

First published 2016

Manufactured in the United States

ISBN 978.1.46711.959.7
Library of Congress Control Number: 2016939298

For Walter McMiller Jr. and, with love, for Yvette and Nettie on his behalf.

CONTENTS

FOREWORD

Reporters walk a fine line whenever we're covering tragic events. Sometimes it's the worst day of someone's life when we're at the front door or on the phone, asking for a comment. So when the tables are turned and the reporter becomes the story, the role reversal tells you a lot about character.

That's how I met Jean Bolduc, when her contract job as a local columnist at Durham's *Herald-Sun* was about to be eliminated as the paper changed hands. She went to the newspaper's headquarters as our cameras rolled and, standing in the driveway, let us know what the loss of those voices that chronicled local history meant to the community. Then, still committed to assisting that community, she started handling press relations for the city's housing authority. And she kept writing, kept talking to people whose stories didn't always make headlines, kept listening to those who experienced the evolution of this region from the old South to a place that keeps appearing on those lists of Best Places to Live.

You're holding the result of her experiences in your hands. It's the unvarnished story of two of the Research Triangle's well-known corners, Durham and Chapel Hill, as told by the people who lived through the years of institutional as well as blatant racism that meant denied opportunities.

Jean, who grew up in New England, didn't know much about those challenges until the Klan marched through Chapel Hill, but the experience led her to a life behind keyboards with her ear to the ground and empathy for those whose candor made this book possible.

Share these stories.

Anthony Wilson
Anchor/Reporter, ABC 11 Eyewitness News
Durham, North Carolina

PREFACE

These stories will be lost.

I became friends with Walter McMiller Jr. when he and I worked together at the Durham Housing Authority. I was the corporate communications director, and Walter was the agency's internal auditor and compliance manager. It's hard to explain how people become friends, really. For me, it's usually the spark of sharing the same point of view in a funny moment.

One such moment that stands out was a Monday morning senior staff meeting on March 5, 2007, following a Duke-Carolina basketball game. This particular matchup left Tyler Hansbrough, a UNC legend-in-the-making, with a broken, bloody nose after Duke's Gerald Henderson's elbow collided with Hansbrough's face. There was great discussion during the game as to whether this was merely a personal foul or a thrown punch—a flagrant foul with greater penalty.

Carolina won the game decisively, and Henderson sat on the bench for Duke's next outing—which was in the ACC tournament.

I arrived in our boss's office for our staff meeting, and as we all took our places around the conference table, I put down my materials and at the perfect moment announced, "It was a PUNCH." The table erupted into a lively discussion that derailed the meeting for several minutes and had Walter and me in stitches.

Walter is African American. I am white. Our veins run Carolina blue. We'd often have lunch together and have some pretty lively discussions about politics—local and national—and sports, of course. The unusual

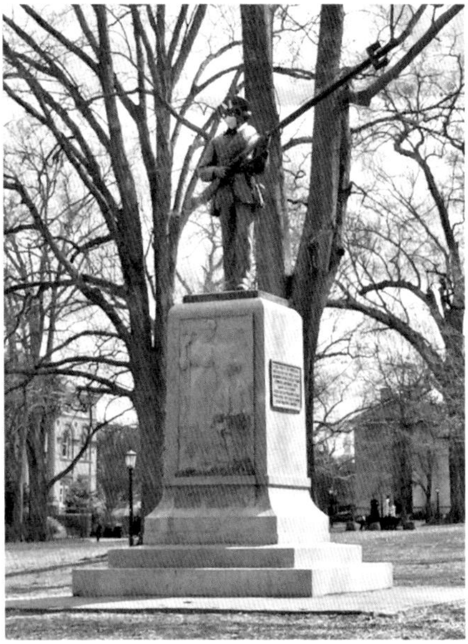

On the day after a UNC win over Duke in ACC basketball, Carolina's "Silent Sam" Confederate memorial becomes a playful symbol of a great athletic rivalry. *Photograph by the author.*

thing was, we would often delve into the topic that is so uncomfortable for many. We would talk about race. We talked about it a lot. We found it fascinating and rich with cultural information previously unavailable for each of us. Our fascination with this exploration ran deep.

We both left our employment with the housing authority, but our friendship endured. We had a whole world of things to talk about that had nothing to do with the work we had been doing. Many more stories to tell.

Something happened to both of us when UNC coach Dean Smith died in the spring of 2015. We heard in the coverage all about Chapel Hill, so often affectionately referred to as the "Southern Part of Heaven." As Walter would discuss this with me, he would talk about the untold story of the "other part" of Chapel Hill—not so much heaven, but very much southern.

He talked about his experience in growing up in Chatham County, but oriented toward Chapel Hill as his home. His father worked as a groundskeeper for UNC and would often get tickets to games from Coach Smith himself. As a student at UNC, as an undergraduate and while earning his master's degree in public administration, Walter talked about working at Slugs at the Pines restaurant in exchange for food (steaks and the like) that he was permitted to bring home. He struggled financially. He worked hard to graduate from Carolina. And he has about a thousand stories about his experiences living in and near Chapel Hill as well as some time in Savannah, Georgia.

Walter isn't just African American; he is a very dark-skinned man. There's no "passing" (being mistaken for white) for him. Like his complexion, some of his stories about his treatment on account of that complexion are very dark indeed.

As we watched various racially charged events unfold across the United States in 2015, we talked about working together on a project. We talked about telling some of those stories to create some sense of balance when we all talk about how things were in Durham and Orange Counties in the 1960s and 1970s (before I came to North Carolina), how they are now and where they might be going as our communities catch up to our interest. We talked about peeling back the layers and really understanding each other from a racial perspective.

These stories, he said, are going to be lost otherwise. With Smith's passing, we both sensed a clock ticking. Life is short. If you've got something important to share, you'd best get on with it.

It was our plan that I would not only interview Walter for this book, but that he would work with me in securing interviews with others. The truth is, it might have been a whole series of books.

When I e-mailed Walter for a second time to confirm a lunch date in late May, I got a response from his wonderful wife, Yvette, telling me that Walter had suffered a stroke and was in Duke Hospital, fighting for his life. When I visited, I joked that Coach K was walking down Franklin Street in broad daylight. I needed to laugh on his behalf.

And so as Walter has been doing his work to recover, I have sought to do mine in going ahead with "our" project. Most of the oral histories on these pages are the result of interviews that I conducted, but some are not. The interviews with Floyd McKissick Sr., Jackie Wagstaff and Nate Davis are part of the Southern Oral History Project at the University of North Carolina at Chapel Hill, which I commend to you as a reader. This is a database of some amazing material.

In these chapters, you find relatively little narration. There's no need to interrupt a great story told by someone who was there, though sometimes it's helpful to fill in some details.

To keep the conversation going and collect more stories, please visit jeanbolduc.com.

ACKNOWLEDGEMENTS

My immense gratitude goes to the University of North Carolina at Chapel Hill for the use of the interviews collected via the Southern Oral History Program. Our universities do amazing work in preserving our culture, history and all the details of our lives. If you're like me and have to set an alarm to roust yourself out of being lost in the time travel of historical documents, you'll understand my sense that it was Christmas in July when I discovered the UNC-CH database containing untold numbers of interviews, both in audio and transcribed form. What a gift.

My thanks to Lynn Richardson, the local history librarian for her assistance in securing an image from the Durham County Collection. Also, my gratitude to the *News & Observer* for permission to use two photographs from the archives for this work.

Hug a librarian.

Interview with Floyd McKissick, Sr. by Bruce Kalk, May 31, 1989, L-0040, in the Southern Oral History Program Collection #4007, Southern Historical Collection, Wilson Library, University of North Carolina at Chapel Hill.

Interview with Nate Davis by Bob Gilgor, February 6, 2001, K-0538, in the Southern Oral History Program Collection #4007, Southern Historical Collection, Wilson Library, University of North Carolina at Chapel Hill.

Interview with Jackie Wagstaff by Alicia Rouverol, December 1, 1998, K-0145, in the Southern Oral History Program Collection #4007, Southern Historical Collection, Wilson Library, University of North Carolina at Chapel Hill.

1

FLOYD MCKISSICK

There has to be a method of opening the doors. I still believe that there is a need for direct action in many areas today.

We begin with Floyd B. McKissick Sr., a civil rights leader, attorney, husband, father and distinguished North Carolinian. He was born in Asheville, North Carolina, in 1922 and was interviewed on May 31, 1989, by Bruce Kalk of the University of North Carolina at Chapel Hill as part of the university's Southern Oral History Program. He died of lung cancer in 1991 soon after being appointed a state district court judge in the Ninth Judicial District by Republican governor Jim Martin.

His father was Ernest Boice McKissick of Kelton, (Union County) South Carolina. The McKissicks, he said, had been on the McKissick plantations "down there from slavery all the way on." His parents met and married at Livingston College (Methodist) in Salisbury, North Carolina. Floyd was the second child of four children and the only boy. His parents finished "normal school" (teachers' college). They were hardworking people.

A grandson of ministers, McKissick said he enjoyed a strong religious influence growing up, with his church providing social structure and a lot of activities in his segregated community.

Asheville, North Carolina, is a tourist town, and my father did hotel work and also worked for North Carolina Mutual Life Insurance Company, which was a fledgling company. He was an agent for North Carolina Mutual Life Insurance Company. Mother could sew. We had a sign on the house: "Seamstress."

She could sew very well and make all kinds of clothes. Made my clothes, of which I was real proud of, one of my first suits. She worked at a department store in Asheville at one time. And then she went back to school and took a business course and then went to work for North Carolina Mutual Life Insurance Company. She began as a cashier-clerk. She worked there until she retired. My father, on the other hand, worked at North Carolina Mutual and the hotels.

He later went into the government service. I think at the time that he died he was with the Veteran's Administration. I don't know how much to tell you about their backgrounds, but I had good parents. There's no way that I can blame anything—that any of the children could ever say anything about their parents didn't try to do for them. Our parents did. Can't blame them for anything. They helped us go to school. They pushed us through school. We were taught to sacrifice to support the family, to go to church, to do what was right, and what was wrong, we were punished if we didn't do it. I would think that some of my very early years, my childhood, my family life as a child in Asheville, were some of my very, very happy years. So I can't complain about that part of my life. I think the struggle parts of my life were [caused by] the fact that I was black, which oft times interfered with so much of the happiness that I might be enjoying when there's some abrupt change would come about, to tell you that you were black and not wanted. I think most of my fights as a child came about issues growing out of that.

I had elementary school teachers who taught me all of the basics, and I remember all of them basically knew my name. I can remember all my school teachers who taught me. I think that teachers were more committed in that day. I think some of the bitter experiences that I had were, that I remember quicker than any other experiences, was the fact that I was skating. We had a street on which we skated in Asheville, a very smooth street, South French Broad, at which time I was assigned by my scout master to direct traffic and help the smaller kids. We were told to get out in an intersection, and the scout master had just placed us in the intersection to keep the smaller kids from coming through the intersection. Some cops came up and said get off the street. We didn't have no business being there. And in trying to explain to them, they proceeded to beat and slap me around a little bit, and I retaliated by throwing a skate.

McKissick described his attempt (with the NAACP) to request that Paul Robeson be permitted to speak at the civic center.

We had to go before the City Council to ask for his permission to speak at the civic center in Asheville in the city auditorium. That was denied. There were many problems of segregation in the city which we were regularly fighting every day, as it related to blacks in a southern city where segregation was prevalent. These incidents arose quite frequently.

As a child, we had many incidents of my riding on the front of the bus to watch the driver, and then my aunt telling me that I couldn't sit up there. And while she was explaining to me, some big heavy man, weighing about 300 pounds, told her if she couldn't get me up, he was going to pick me up and throw me to the rear of the bus. I then got up and went back to the back of the trolley car. I said bus. It was really a trolley car. Asheville had trolley cars. This was on Montclair trolley car that I remember this. And my aunt picked me up and took me to the back, and she just cried as she sat there with me. I sort of got the understanding of what things were all about a little later in life, not then. I can remember other incidents of that type also.

In 1939, McKissick left Asheville to go to Morehead College in Atlanta, Georgia, and then worked in Connecticut for a summer on a tobacco farm. He left the army in 1945 and was in and out of school, depending on his finances. Tuition, he recalled, was about $325 a year. Service in Europe changed the perspective of many soldiers from the segregated South. They could see a world without it. McKissick and his fellow veterans discovered that while World War II was over, the battle for equality at home was just beginning.

We wrote and asked for applications right after I came out of the army in '45 requesting admission. We never received a reply to our first letter to the University of North Carolina. I was living in Asheville then. A short time before that there was the Hocutt case which had been brought to go to the University of North Carolina. Raymond Hocutt, I think, was his name, who had tried to go to North Carolina, and I think that that case was tried in state court and was lost. And he was not permitted to get into the case.

My association, after we got out of the army, we were determined that there was not going to be any more segregation in North Carolina. I think most of the fellows who had been in World War II had been around the world, and they had seen things, and they knew that they were not what America had depicted them to be. They had seen the whole world, and they were not going to live in a pattern of segregation as they had in the past.

When we came to North Carolina, I went to Morehouse and did another year. I had three years of college under my belt, and I had made the Dean's List at Morehouse. The Dean's List was what we called the honor roll. I came up to

North Carolina Central. At that time it was called North Carolina College for Negroes, or they had just changed it to North Carolina College at Durham. I was admitted to law school, and we immediately decided upon getting the law school accredited. It was unaccredited. Didn't have enough books. Didn't have enough space. Didn't have enough facilities. It was called the law department.

The Need for Action

We then went to the legislature. Efforts to talk to people didn't prove to any avail, so we decided to picket the legislature. At that time the newspaper didn't pick up too much of what black people wanted to negotiate, no way. You had to take some action. The only time that they would listen to you was some action. We decided to picket the legislature. So a group of us picketed the legislature, and as a result of picketing the legislature, they decided to expend more money to bring the law school up to accredited levels. We also decided that we needed to bring, with the cooperation of NAACP, suit to enter the University of North Carolina.

Talk was going on that maybe they would let somebody in over there. Some quiet talk never proved to be of any benefit. But we did picket. Before we brought the suit, I was not the first plaintiff. I think I was about the third in line. There was Harold Epps and [Robert David] Glass and there was another person who was in the law suit and ended up.... Epps graduated and someone else stepped down from the suit, and I became the major plaintiff in the suit after that time. Then after I became the major plaintiff, at the time the case was being called for trial, there were interveners. The interveners were Jay Kenneth Lee, Harvey Beech, Eugene Lassiter, and possibly four or more others who joined just before the suit started trial in Durham.

McKissick v. Carmichael, 1950

We had attempted to—after we get out of the army, I knew that I was going into law. And during the time that I was in Atlanta we had written the University of North Carolina and gotten no reply to asking them. It was generally felt—there was a feeling in the air that people were going to be fair and treat you right. You were a returning veteran, and some schools were letting blacks in that never had before. There were high quotas, and veterans

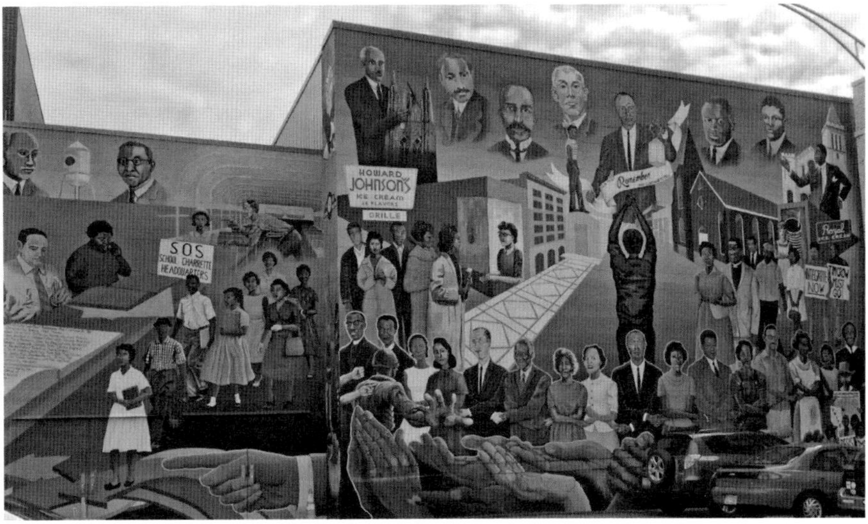

Durham today: A civil rights history mural titled *We Must Remember and Continue to Tell* highlighting many signature events, including the Howard Johnson's protest in 1962. The mural (the work of Brenda Miller Holmes) is located behind the Durham Convention Center, on Morris Street beside the Durham Arts Council. *Photograph by the author.*

were getting quotas. So there was a feeling in North Carolina...that North Carolina would do some of these things without being forced to do it.

That feeling was later determined to be a false feeling, false emotion, that we had. And after I came to the law school here and I saw. The best thing that North Carolina Central had was some good professors, solid professors, who were teaching, and they were really giving you everything that they had. But we didn't have the books, and they used to always say, "We do not have these books. We do not have this and that. And you will have to do this." And there was no place for us to go get these things, no place to go, no place to borrow books. We didn't have the Reporters that we needed.

I had made applications to go to law school to about seven law schools and had been admitted to Cleveland, Western Reserve. I think at that time Fordham Law School, I had been admitted. But each one had given you a time to come, and you would have been out of school a half a year because the list was so long. Howard University had a long list. All the black kids in the country were just about going to Howard, and to get on that list you'd have to wait three years before you could get in school.

So it was decided, here's North Carolina right here. We knew that North Carolina Central, the law school there, was not comparable to the University of North Carolina. We had been over there and had seen the University of

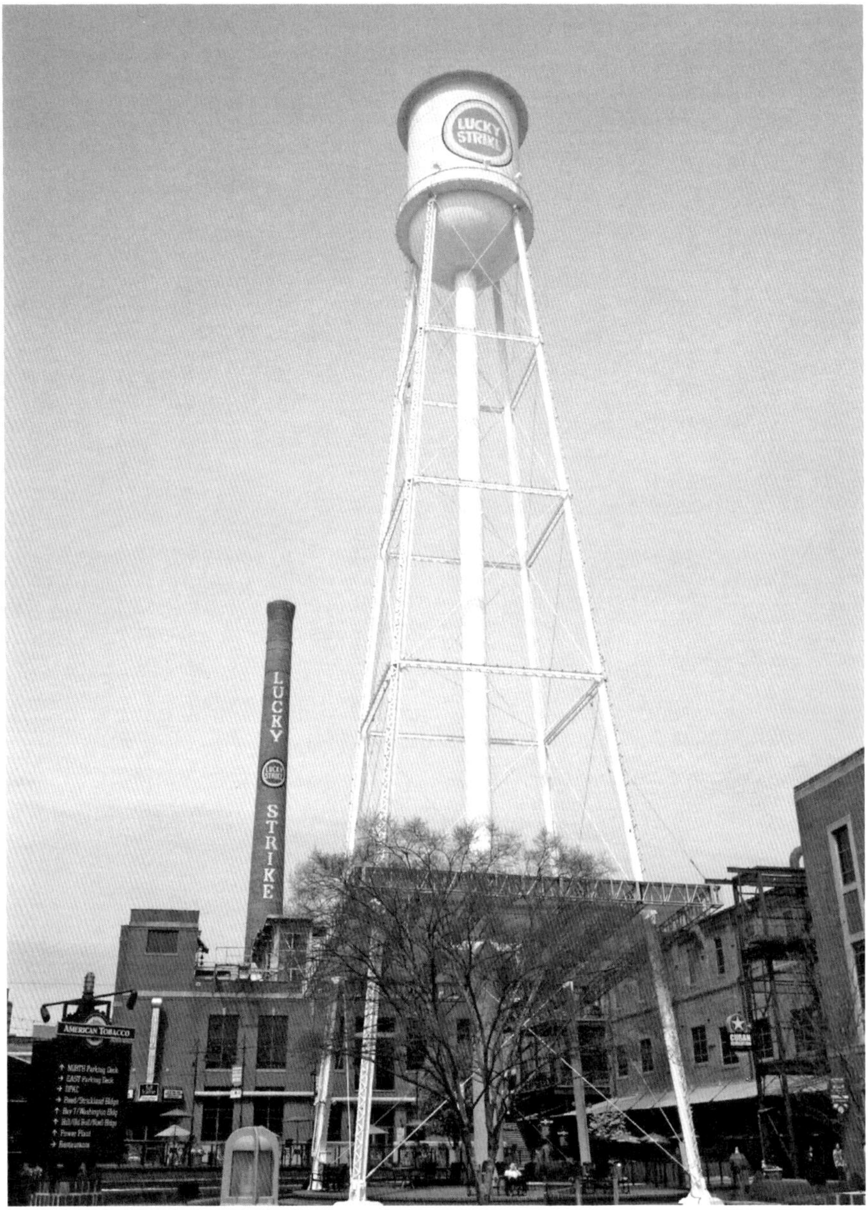

Durham today: The American Tobacco campus in Durham features iconic structures that echo tobacco's past. *Photograph by the author.*

North Carolina and saw the difference. They didn't know what we were doing over there or anything, but we went over to see the difference, and we made these comparisons. At that time the NAACP had done some studies, and we were ready for this suit. It was just decided that suits were being brought all over, in many states in the South, at this time to desegregate the law schools, the professional schools. And we decided that we were going to go ahead and crack the law school and crack it now. It was just, you had top students. We could have got in school anywhere. It was just a matter that we were black, and the University, one of the worst things they were doing was not replying to correspondence or just ignoring it or throwing it away, which had occurred for two years in a row. So it was then decided that a suit was the possible way.

We decided that a law school was going to be the best way. There were some blacks in the community who knew some whites over there, and there had been meetings among those groups of blacks and whites who met together—I think the Southern Conference for Human Welfare at that time, headed by Clark Forman out of New Orleans. There were other black and white groups who met—the Congress of Racial Equality (CORE), the NAACP, black and white church groups, particularly Charles Jones, a white Presbyterian minister of Chapel Hill was one of my strong supporters. Had certainly supported me, and at a time when I really needed the support, was there with me at the University of North Carolina.

While awaiting the decision in his lawsuit to gain admission to UNC School of Law, McKissick went to law school and graduated. Yes, he graduated. Still, he wanted to see through to the end the process for which he was fighting—that he should have been admitted like anyone else and been allowed to attend without fear. So he attended Carolina for a semester.

Progress was slow. Just as courts do today, progress was moving along. I think that it was during my first year of school, getting some of the years straight, my first year of school was the 1949–50 school year at North Carolina Central. And the next year was 1950–51, and so consequently, it takes three years to go to law school, and the decision came about the same week that I graduated and received my degree from North Carolina Central. You see, I had graduated from North Carolina Central Law School.

I was the plaintiff, and Thurgood Marshall was our attorney, who told me at that time to go to the University of North Carolina because my grades, they were questioning the grades of students, and they were making many questions. He said, "I don't believe that you'll have any difficulty over there at all.

I believe your grades are straight, and I believe that you can make the course." There were rumors that if anybody came over there, they weren't going to pass, no way. They were going to fail them. And [Marshall] said, "I believe that you can understand it, and you can take the pressure and the stress." That was the reason that I went over, although I had completed by legal requirements at that time. I still went to the University for that summer—just for that summer.

The "Unwelcome" Mat

Snakes, Buckets of Water and Threats from the Klan

Since McKissick was going to UNC–Chapel Hill to prove a point, he proved it everywhere possible. He was not looking to make a spectacle of himself. To the contrary, he was looking to demonstrate that he was a guy going to law school—just like his classmates.

Some of the students did not live on the campus. I was one of the ones that lived on campus in a cubicle up there at Steele Hall, I think. I was also a working student, and I waited tables at a place called the Barlett House. And working at the Barlett House out there, I would work in the evenings. My job would start at about five o'clock, and it would be over with around about one or two o'clock at night, and then I'd come in and go to bed and get up. So consequently, sometimes I was the only black student on the campus. I was the only black there many a day. There was an honor system in existence then. No doors were locked, and I didn't lock my doors. I stayed in a cubicle where the other black students were supposed to stay and did stay sometimes during the day time. Many of them didn't want to at night.

So I was alone there. And they would come in and they'd put a black snake in my drawer, a dead black snake, in my drawer on my shirts. They would put water on your clothes. Put a bucket of water over your door to trick you. When you came in, you opened the door, a bucket of water would fall. Because, see, no doors were locked. They would be half-way or partially open. They had a lot of fun with you. They thought they were having fun. You'd get a letter every day from the Ku Klux Klan telling you that you're at the wrong place and what's going to happen to you. You had a lot of threats.

I, however, didn't let the threats bother me too much. And when I came in, I'd study. Classes started, I think, at 7:30 or 8:00. I would be in my class, and I'd be ready to go. And then that summer, I think that things were segregated around the campus. I had to establish my right to eat in Steele Hall dining room.

That was Lenoir Hall, I think, dining room. After two or three kids knocked the trays out of my hand, I went through the line one day and made the big announcement that, "I intend to eat today, and I don't intend to let anybody knock any tray out of my hand anymore. I can't afford it in the first place." And I walked through that line and didn't nobody say nothing. And I stopped all that.

I never had any trouble sitting at the library. There were some incidents of some of the kids went to the swimming pool to swim, and they wouldn't let them in. I told them this pool was going to get integrated today, and I just went on and jumped into the pool. After I jumped into the pool, I walked on out and nobody said anything to me, and I said nothing to anybody else. I said, "It's integrated now." And that was it. No one ever said anything to me about it or anything. I got soaking wet but it was so hot that day that I got dry. But that was about all that occurred.

Anne Queen was the lady who was at the YMCA, who certainly gave us support the whole time. There were a number of students. Don't forget the pressure on many of the white students that would try to treat us nice, were called "nigger lovers." But there were always a group of whites there who wanted us there, and who tried to help us out in many ways. But they were under a great amount of pressure, and some evenings they would come by and talk to me. When I got there late at night, quite often there would be somebody to talk to me, so long as no one was around to harass them, call them a "nigger lover" for their associating with me. That was one of the major problems that was going on any time someone would try to befriend you or treat you nice and pick up a book for you. There would always be a little choir around to holler, "Nigger lover, nigger lover, nigger lover," and that stopped many of the whites from trying to do anything.

McKissick described UNC's reputation for liberalism (despite these incidents) this way:

I think you had a man like Frank Porter Graham who expressed himself nationally, and there were members on the faculty who had expressed themselves that we knew about. There were always people at the University of North Carolina who disagreed with the policies of segregation even when I went there, before we had arrived. There were people who talked with us, who gave us advice on what to do and how to do it, and who were friendly. But the basic, it's a political school and it was a political process that tied up so many of the minds of those who were there. I would like to think that it was primarily political rather than…I think the academic community, well, I'd say at least fifty percent of the academic community, didn't care one way or the other. But I would think that it was basically political. And because it's involved in the politics of North Carolina, it was not going to improve any faster than any other process in the state.

I do recall that just before we were getting ready to take exams in the course that I was taking—and it was taught by Professor Voight, who was said to be a German, who taught us sales. About a week before, I had been in sales class and had been called upon to speak, answer questions, and I'd always answer pretty correctly. I kept up with my homework even though I was working. And just before we got ready to take the examination, about a week before, one night I came up to my room and a couple of fellows were in the room, and we started talking about sales, and then a couple of more came in. And about the middle of the summer I think the attitudes had changed. There used to be a choir who used to holler "nigger lover." During the summer I think that it was prevalent on a regular basis. But by the end of the summer it had faded down. And then the kids in my class, who came in the room to study with me, said, "You know, we want to study with you because we think that we can help each other." They had reached that point. And I began to feel much better. I knew then that I certainly had lost a lot of the inferiority complex that I had previously had.

I was the first one in a sense, but there were others during this summer session. This was the only session where there were blacks. With me at that time I think was Lassiter, taking that class. There was another class in which another black was in. I think that Lenoir Hall—had received its first black and then it was over with. I think they have to go through the first black syndrome. It's a syndrome for white people. Have you ever seen a black eat. They think all kinds of things. I think all these stereotypes are thrown out of the window after they undergo their experience with the first black, being associated with them. So I think that those of us who went there first, cleared up the minds of whites more than those of blacks. There were few blacks coming after that. I mean relatively few were coming in. But the door had been made easier for them. Sometimes you found it difficult to study. It did take people who were really ready to fight who went there first, because they had to make the course and couldn't let things distract them. And there was enough distraction on the basis of race and what people would say, and some of the authorities didn't try to help you out. And maybe one professor would be nice and speak, but many of them wouldn't speak for failure to get peer approval.

Making Friends

I think one of the friends that I made was Dan Pollock at the University of North Carolina Law School. His family and my family are tight friends today, Dan Pollock. We were both newly married. We both raised our children. Our children grew up basically together. We were in every organization for the protection or promotion of rights, civil rights, in particular, first amendment rights, freedom of speech. We share Christmas parties, weddings, and anniversaries. That's one of the best friends I ever had, I met at the University of North Carolina, was Dan Pollock.

I think the number of students in the 1960s that came in increased dramatically, and they only brought in a number of students after they hired blacks to develop a program to bring in more students, into the University of North Carolina. I think when federal funds became available on a non-discriminatory basis, the University decided that they wanted federal funds, and they decided to recruit more blacks also.

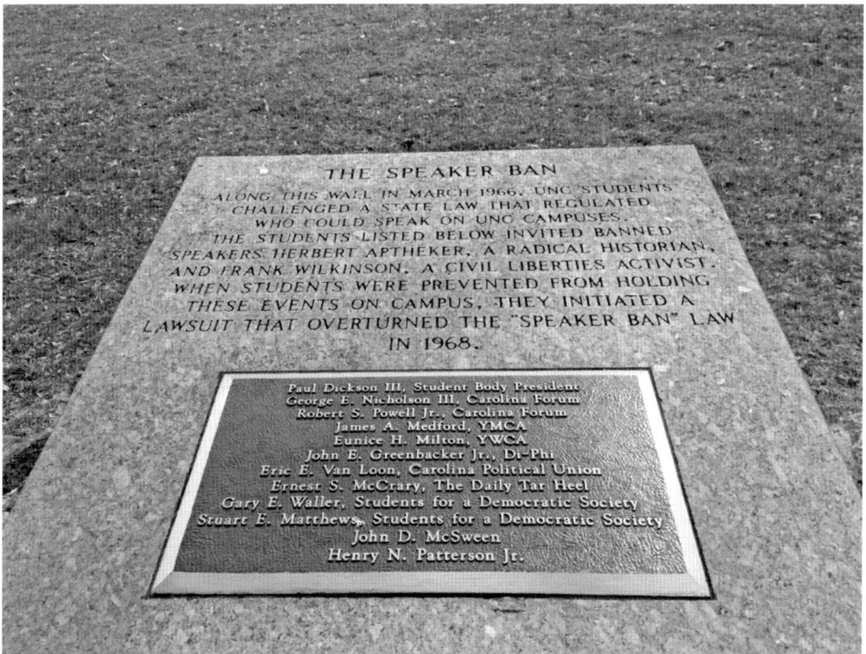

A marker on the stone wall of the UNC campus recalls free speech protests from the 1960s. *Photograph by the author.*

I think that the University has made progress in many ways. I think it still needs to concentrate on establishing a policy of full integration. It has not established a policy of full integration. I think it's been applying the oil where the squeak was in the wheel. If you don't really holler, nothing is corrected. There has to be pressure brought about before corrections are made. I wish that all of the universities, not only UNC, but Duke as well, would decide to get more faculty persons and administration and at all levels of the development and growth of the university. It would be far more meaningful to blacks than just having black students. And I think they need to go out and recruit and bring in far more black students than they do.

North Carolina has always been able to hide, to a great extent—or put forth, is what I should say, rather than hide—I think they've put forth a public relations image that they are far more progressive than other southern states. But I think that if you look at the record now, you've got far more black elected officials in Alabama and Mississippi and far more legislations to carry out federal programs in Mississippi and Alabama than you have in North Carolina to date. In particular, when it comes to economic development toward blacks, Mississippi has passed some special legislation. And Alabama, even under Governor Wallace, had changed its course and actions towards blacks, and it opened up doors for employment. Both of these states would now compare and exceed the numbers in schools and educational institutions than North Carolina even today.

I thought one time I ought to place an application over there to teach, now that I'm about ready to retire. See if they would offer me a job. See if they're ready to say that, you know, the time is come, and we're going to do it.

I think I've always been an activist in the civil rights movement. That started from the incident where I was beaten by the cops, I was telling you about, in Asheville, North Carolina. I have been active in demonstrations. I believe in civil disobedience, and I believe that if you believe the law is wrong, then you disobey that law and you pay the consequences for it. And I believe that you have to resort to demonstrations where you have the lack of response to requests or lack of communications. There has to be a method of opening the doors. So there's no other method except an outward confrontation, and that confrontation has to be had and has to be had in public in order to bring about change. I still believe that. I still believe that there's a need for direct action in many areas today.

I'm associated with the University of North Carolina through the regional planning school. My son went to school over there. My daughter went to undergraduate school at Carolina, and my son went to the School of Planning and got his Master's degree. I see the University as a great thing. I think it's able to do far more than it does though. It has a great amount of power. It doesn't seem to use its power to bring about the changes that can be made, or to tie the town and gown together. On the other hand, there are individuals, and there have always been a number of individual professors who have always championed the cause of blacks or minorities or the underprivileged. And the University still has that spark in it which I love to support whenever I see that spark coming in from the students or from the professors over there. Every liberal movement, I think, in the state of North Carolina has been associated—there have been professors from the University of North Carolina associated with it. I'm talking about white professors who have been associated with it. The University could do a lot more than what it's doing though.

2

WALTER JACKSON

In many of his actions as a young man, Floyd McKissick Sr. had in mind how he could benefit those who followed behind him and stood on his shoulders. Walter Jackson of Durham is a gentleman whose footprints rest squarely on McKissick's shoulders, and he is grateful to stand there.

He was born in Kings Mountain, North Carolina (southwest of Charlotte), in the mid-1940s and spent his first decade there. Walter Jackson's father worked for one of the first black radio stations in the Durham area, selling advertising. He is the youngest of three, with two older sisters. I asked him how that went for him (being the youngest), and his response was elegant in its simplicity and good humor. "I didn't like it," he said.

His parents did not finish high school but were well read. His mother had a number of jobs—she cooked in a restaurant in Kings Mountain and worked as a maid in a home in Durham. The radio station owner hired Jackson's mother to work in his home.

Jackson is a person whose personal integrity and sheer decency could cause anyone to underestimate his tenacity and sense of direction. There is no doubt that among his most endearing characteristics is his sense of humor. He is always ready with a joke or the memory of a song that is evocative of the events of the day. Rather than a simple compliment of appreciation like "thanks for your help on that project," he is more likely to say, "I'm reminded of a wonderful song that says 'If they gave me a fortune, my pleasure would be small, I could lose it all tomorrow and never mind at all, but if I should lose your love dear, I don't know what I'd do—for I know I'll never find another you.'"

Why bother with a simple thank-you when you can bring the Seekers along with you?

Walter Jackson attended Durham schools under segregation, graduating from Hillside High School in 1963. Thanks to McKissick's paving the way a decade prior with his law school admission, Jackson was admitted to UNC–Chapel Hill to major in journalism. With graduation came a trip to Vietnam—an experience Jackson says he feels fortunate to have survived. And then, an unexpected detour to Cambridge, Massachusetts.

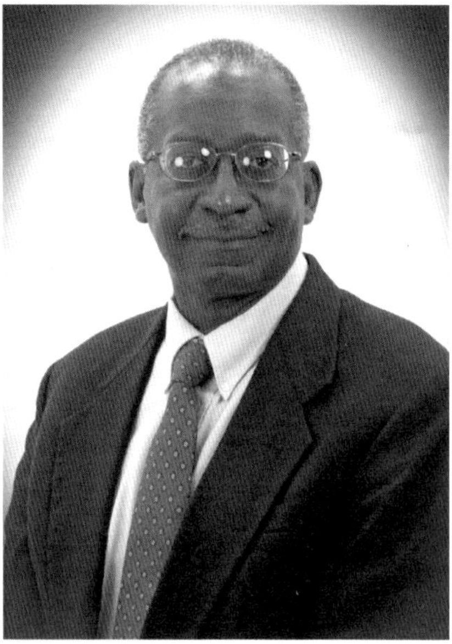

Walter Jackson. *Courtesy of Walter Jackson.*

LAW ENFORCEMENT

I asked Jackson if he had ever been arrested. He smiled sheepishly (and one could hardly imagine him being in trouble) and said "Oh, no, no . . ." but then recalled his one experience in handcuffs.

In 1963, spring of my senior year (in high school), I did have an experience with law enforcement that landed me in the Durham County jail. There was a large civil rights demonstration at the Howard Johnson's restaurant that was located on the Durham/Chapel Hill Boulevard. My recollection is that, on that day, more than seven hundred people were locked up and my sisters and I were among that number.

They rounded us up, took us to jail. I don't recall if I was in jail for the whole night or not, but the charges were dropped.

I was scared. Any number of things could have happened. A number of good old boys were along the road with shotguns. Anything could have happened.

We had been coached for what to do. Told to "go limp" which would make it more difficult to move us.

Our parents did not know in advance, but they understood what we were doing.

We were trained by local leaders of civil rights movement, in particular attorney Floyd McKissick, who was leading the Congress of Social Equality and Ben Ruffin.

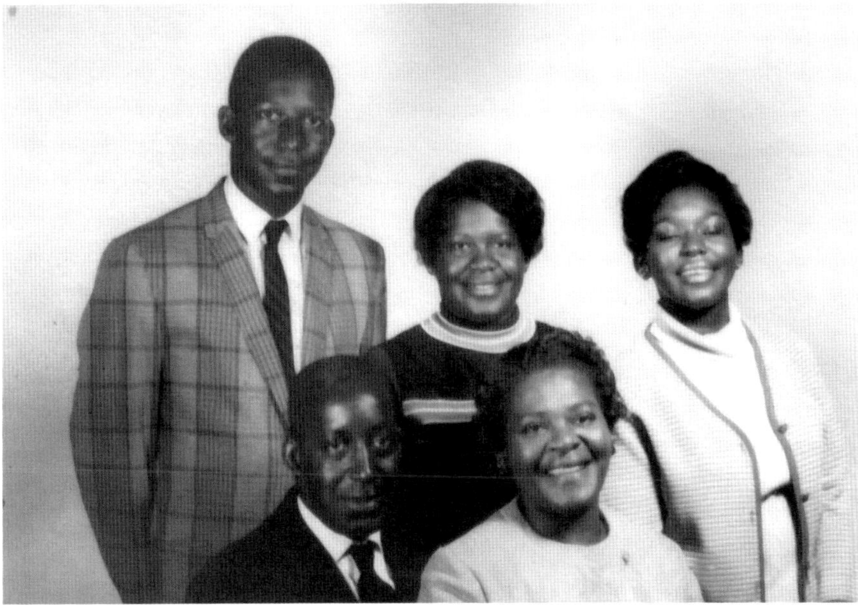

Walter Jackson with his parents and sisters. *Courtesy of Walter Jackson.*

When we think of think of the civil rights era, iconic images of conflict and confrontation come to mind. Jackson describes his experience a bit differently:

Confrontation with police wasn't that much in the public eye as it is now. We lived in a black community, not much interaction with whites. More integration meant more opportunities for conflict.

The community I lived in was very comfortable to me. Didn't feel protected but didn't feel threatened either. I walked to and from school in the Hayti community. I was comfortable wherever I needed to go.

I was one of the first African Americans to be admitted to the J-School (UNC School of Journalism) and the third to graduate. During that time… the murder of Emmett Till, George Wallace was trying to keep the schools segregated. North Carolina was a bit more advanced than other states in the South. UNC admitted its first African American student to the law school in 1952. I wasn't admitted until 1963. By then, there were very few African American students on campus, but there wasn't the rioting like they did at Ole Miss.

In his first semester at UNC, Jackson learned of the assassination of President Kennedy, an event that struck fear in the hearts of every American. Though a college student, Jackson was still living with his parents in Durham. "I was outside Bingham Hall waiting for my next class," he recalled. "Someone ran up and told me. I went on to class. I was commuting at that time. Later on, I drove home and brought another student home."

Two days later, he watched the murder of Lee Harvey Oswald on live television.

Vietnam

I had been in the Air Force ROTC and was going to enter after graduation as an officer, but failed the physical exam. I was drafted into the army, was able to get that overturned, finished my college career, then enlisted in Officer Candidate School in the Signal Corps. While in basic, they called out everyone in Signal Corps, said you need to go into artillery or infantry instead.

Then I was off to Fort Benning, Georgia, for Officer Candidate School (OCS). I didn't want to be a platoon leader. Because of training I had received, they saw fit to send me to Vietnam, but once there (after three months) got into the Public Information Office—a much better life for being in the field. We would do stories for soldiers' hometown papers. Sometimes we'd have to go out into the field where a battle had just occurred and write about it.

After I left OCS I was left with only a two-year commitment—twenty-one months. They had a policy that if you only had ninety days or less in your enlistment, they'd release you. So I was done.

I had interned at the *Durham Morning Herald* while I was at Chapel Hill and they would give me a job when I came back from Vietnam. So I thought I would start a career as a journalist. I guess I hadn't thought very far in advance. Growing up in North Carolina, when I was going to school in Chapel Hill I had made the statement "I don't like big cities. I don't like cold weather and I never want to live outside the South."

A few months after getting back from Vietnam I found myself in big, dirty, cold Pittsburgh, Pennsylvania. And I found myself in a number of other Northern cities and other big cities—Charlotte, Atlanta, Cleveland, Boston (for a school year) and Salt Lake City. So I've made my peace with big cities.

I've been back in Durham in Chapel Hill area for about a decade now and appreciate "the green, green grass of home." That song was very big with the soldiers in Vietnam.

Harvard

In high school I was a very good student but with all that was happening with me and around me when I was a student in Chapel Hill, I was just sort of a good student who graduated with a "thank you, lawdy" (rather than summa cum laude).

My career took a number of interesting turns including the opportunity to work for the City of Durham for five years as the city's public information officer. In 1982, I was working in Cleveland, Ohio, for Standard Oil Company and I had friends who made me aware of a program at Harvard where you could earn a master's degree that was available for people with five years of experience in the public sector. And you could do this in one school year.

And I said "Oh well Harvard would never admit me." They encouraged me to apply and I thought well I'll apply but I don't know why I'm wasting my time…I'll never get in. Sometime around Labor Day in 1982 my family and I came back to Durham for a week or so on vacation. When I got back to Cleveland and got my mail there was a letter from Harvard. It was in a large envelope and I thought—it only takes a small envelope to say "get out of here," but to my surprise I had been admitted. Even though I got this letter a little over a week before school started, I went to work the next day and said "I've been admitted to Harvard and I'm going. I'd like a leave of absence from the job and I'd like financial support and I know they only have a week to do this and you only have a week to make the decision." In fact, the company did come through in a big way. They didn't pay my tuition but they did grant me a leave of absence and allow me to come back.

And then there I was at Harvard—a place I never expected to even be able to walk across the campus yet there I was.

Local Politics

Growing up, even though I was a voracious reader local politics was not something I was very interested in.

I was interested in how the world works. Over the years I've been exposed to a number of great thinkers, speakers in politics, business and economics. I just realize the importance of being actively involved. At some point in the 1980s I threw my hat in the ring for city council in Durham. I was also struggling trying to start a business so I withdrew from the politics, but I've become involved in trying to get other candidates ready to seek office. I became involved in the Durham Committee for the Affairs of Black People which is a very important political organization in the city of Durham. Recently served a term as chair of the political committee. It was very energizing.

Jackson is a man who can get along with just about anyone. He has the remarkable gift of an easygoing personality, tremendous wit, intellect and an accompanying humility that is rare among people who are as sharp as he is. With his unusual ability to embrace and celebrate the dignity and accomplishments of others with sincerity and real meaning, a necessary question for him was to ask how we might bring our diverse society closer together, focusing on our common interests and not magnifying our differences. Again, Jackson recalls a song that is right on point.

I wish I had the answer to what does it take to see how you could do better people could just get along.

Despite the efforts of a lot of people over all these years I don't know that things are a lot better than they were when I was growing up, some things got better some things got worse. There was a popular song "What the World Needs Now Is Love"…it almost comes down to that, but how that's going to happen or if that's going to happen, I have no idea. One would think that religion could and should be the answer but that doesn't seem to be the case.

I have been involved in my church. I had two parents who believed in not only sending their children to church but taking their children to church. So I was at church either every Sunday or almost every Sunday. I'd be at church on Sunday night for church service or Bible school and over the summer or frequently at prayer meetings on Wednesday nights. I had a very much church-oriented childhood. I thought a lot about going to church at Chapel Hill and I thought "I'm not gonna let them shake me of my rigid religious beliefs," but the exposure caused me to change the way I look at some things.

I'm a member at White Rock. The physical location of the church changed because of urban renewal from where it used to be in the center of the Hayti community, but it's the same White Rock Baptist Church.

Marriage and Family

When I came back from Vietnam I said, "Oh my goodness while I was away at college and then in Vietnam everybody got married!" The city editor at the

Durham Morning Herald had been a classmate of mine and his sister-in-law worked at the Department of Social Services. We were talking one day and they put together this single African-American male that he knew and the single African-American female that she knew and they put us together.

We got married and had a wonderful son. Our marriage did not work out, and I've been divorced for a number of years now. My son is Marcus Jackson, born in Charlotte while I was a reporter for the *Charlotte Observer*, and he moved with my wife and me to Atlanta and then on to Cleveland, Ohio. He finished high school here in North Carolina and Halifax County and attended undergraduate school the University of North Carolina at Greensboro. He got a law degree at North Carolina Central University and he's now a practicing attorney with three wonderful children.

President Obama's Election

I asked Jackson to describe his reaction at the moment he knew America had elected Barack Obama to the presidency.

Unbelievable. Incredible.

I had not thought that during my lifetime, blacks couldn't be on the city council, schools were segregated. Going from then to the present with an African-American man being president of the United States—just incredible.

To see the changes in the society how people relate to each other the technology up to and including the election of Barack Obama…it's just joy, pride. Many of us thought this certainly would never happen in our lifetime.

Back in the days when civil rights were advancing and along with it women's rights advancing, you'd hear people express things like "You'd think we'd have a woman president." I think the thinking was that we would elect a woman president long before an African-American president. I don't know if it's just happenstance that it worked out that way.

I don't think he's been a great president; I think he's done a creditable job. I know that we've had great presidents in my lifetime—he's been as good as most or better. It's kind of hard to achieve greatness when one of the major figures in Congress announces on the day of your inauguration that obstructing you from doing anything is a top priority.

History will be the judge, but I think John Kennedy was probably a great president and I think he was president during a very difficult time. He certainly sent the country in the right direction that Lyndon Johnson

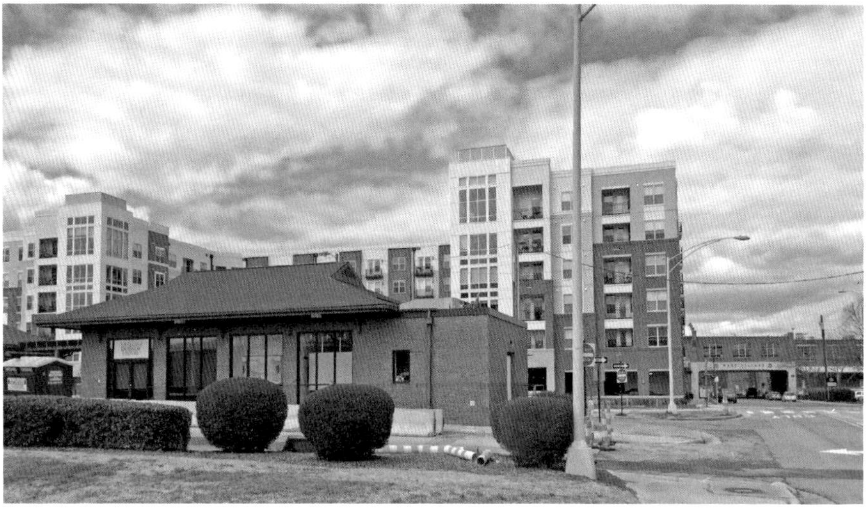

Durham today: The History Hub in downtown Durham features photographic collections and displays of Durham history. Residents can record oral histories in this former train station, which sits just across the tracks from a new housing development and West Village (former tobacco warehouses converted into commercial space). Durham is a city that has reinvented itself from a trading stop for tobacco into a destination location with top-rated restaurants and entertainment venues. *Photograph by the author.*

followed up on with some major legislation—the Civil Rights Act [1964] the Voting Rights Act [1965].

I do feel very, very blessed to be born where I was when I was in 1945 in the rural South to not formally educated parents and to have made it to this point my life, including my getting a college degree and going on to Harvard for master's in a world that I could hardly believe I'd ever have seen. It's just been a tremendous blessing to have seen the amount of social change that has taken place in my life. I've always been committed to trying to do the best I can to take advantage of opportunities, being a good citizen and a good father. I feel incredibly blessed to have come through life and had that experience and still be here and enjoy the blessings I've had along the way. I've traveled all over—while in Vietnam I was able to make excursions to the Philippines and Singapore. When I look back it's been a really, really blessed life.

After watching the funeral service for the victims in the Charleston Emanuel AME Church shooting in June 2015, Jackson said he was rethinking the question of whether or not Obama has been a "great" president. Given his love of music and understanding of its power to persuade, it is likely that the president's wrapping up his remarks with an electrifying performance of "Amazing Grace" moved him to reconsider. After all, if Lincoln was uniquely able to navigate the treacherous political waters of the Civil War, it is surely true that President Barack Obama, a biracial man with a spotless record of personal decency and dignity, could so ably help America confront the scars of racism and white privilege—or at least begin that work.

3

BRENDA STEPHENS

Let me tell you about that bus ride…

Brenda Stephens was born in 1952 in Durham at Duke Hospital. "At the Dukes' Hospital, we called it—for the Duke family owning it," said Stephens. Her father was a farmer, and she grew up living a rural farming life. Her mother went to the Watts School of Nursing in Durham. The farm, which remains Stephens's home, was a place to work and work hard.

I called my mom to go over a few things with her because I was coming to meet with you this morning. Growing up we lived out in the country. We were the country cousins. You know I had cousins who lived in town. We spent the summer walking around, you know my grandfather was a tobacco farmer. The family still owns the land. Dad was the oldest, and they worked the farm.

As a child I spent a lot of time walking around seeing what they were doing—you know I was a girl so I wasn't allowed to do any farming work. I know I wanted to get on the tobacco drag 'cause it look like so much fun. But then we'd be ordered to get back in the house, and I was supposed to watch my grandmother and learn what my grandmother was doing. I thought it was interesting that when it came time to eat, she had an apron on and she'd walk around and she'd have a little something in the apron should be drop in on the ground. She'd be walking out there among these chickens and drop in something on the ground. She'd look and then she just snatch one of those

Right: Brenda Stephens. *Courtesy of Brenda Stephens.*

Below: Mary V. and Charlie Thomas "Rev. Jack" Wilson, Brenda Stephens's grandparents. *Courtesy of Brenda Stephens.*

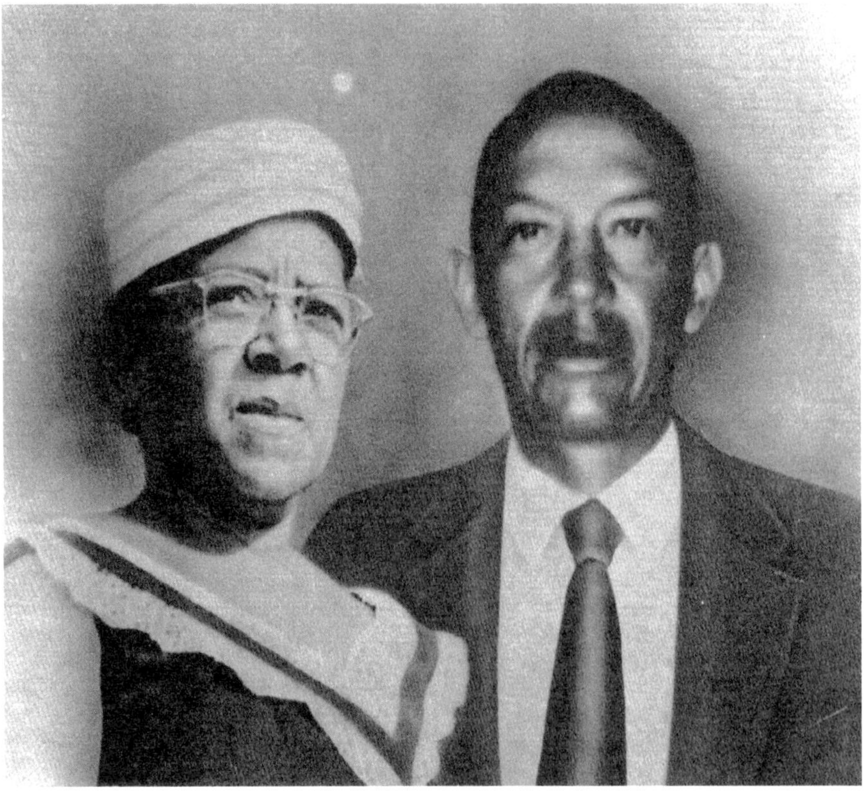

chickens up and wring its neck and it's flopping around, 'n' the next thing I know there's some chicken in some hot water and then it's on the table and she's hollering "Come on for dinner!" And she was plenty fast with it.

Across the road from the house where they would have hog killings and they would drop the hogs off and...ugh. You know when you watch all that stuff you don't really want to be around it that much. Then my mother got this idea that over the summers that we should help our personal growth by sending us away to visit relatives. And I asked Mom about that this morning, and she said, "Well you know, that was my summer vacation."

One summer she sent me to Washington. One summer she sent me to New York. One she sent me to Maryland. And you know she had siblings there. So when I went to D.C., you know, I went to the zoo and I went to the tomb of the unknown soldiers. In New York the little country girl was wowed when I went to Radio City Music Hall—the Rockettes. So I'm there on the bus with my little fried chicken in a bag. Her brother was sitting in another seat and I'm sitting there and you know I'm scared to death and we're going up the road as they called it. Well I felt something and I thought oh no well you know I've got a bad seat. So I told my uncle, "You know there's something wrong with this window; you know there's air coming in here." So he laughed at me and said, "Well you know that's air conditioning."

So my uncle is now about ninety-five or ninety-six, and whenever we get together, they always tell that story.

But the truth is I didn't like going to New York; it's too crowded, there's too many people and it's so huge. And we drive along and someone didn't like the way somebody else was driving and they'd stop and they get out of the car and scream at them, "Where'd you get your license? Sears and Roebuck?" And I'm thinking you know I'm going to get shot or something. I didn't like riding the subways—everybody's gotta hurry up and get on and hurry up and get off. A little companion cousin who was with me always fell in and out of the subway. He was nervous 'cause you know we were told "Are we in or are we out?" You know—don't dillydally.

So no, I didn't like New York then. But you know my mother thought it was for personal growth. That's what she wanted. When she was age eleven, she volunteered to leave home and go live with John Link's aunt—Mertie Walker. She hired her to help out around the house. So thanks to Ms. Mertie, everything was done just so. Mama stayed there from age eleven until she got married. She wanted more.

So when she graduated from high school, she went to the Watts School of Nursing. The Walkers helped her with that.

So I mention something to her today, and I knew she'd be furious. She told me that before schools integrated, public health nurse told her to be on the lookout for them "raising the bar." "And it wasn't mandatory but I went over and signed you up to go to Carrington Jr. High School. A couple of other people in the neighborhood sign their kids up to go too."

The principal told mom when she signed us up that she should plan to drive us to school rather than have us ride the bus. Of course Mom refused. So I told Mama today [summer of 2015] "Let me tell you about that bus ride..."

A few years ago, the bus driver saw me at an outside restaurant in Hillsborough, and he walked up and apologized for not saying something when he was driving that bus about what they were saying to me what they did to me. Mama said, "What did they do?" I told her, "You didn't raise me to be a whiner." I was not going to run home cause my mother worked this shift so that she was in bed asleep when I got home. She would work at night because she could make more money that way. So she would be asleep and I respected that and I was not about to go wake her up and tell her about these things. So today I told her.

There were just a few of us and we had to be the last ones on and so we have to stand up to ride all the way home. So we had a plan that various days, one or two of us would run to the bus to get a seat. So wouldn't always be the same ones who would sprint to get there first. Silly us, we would get a seat in the front. We didn't want to sit in the back. So when we get our seat in the front we get whacked in the back of the head. So we had kind of a choice... we could sit in the back. So if you didn't want to run you could walk to the bus and they had a name for that walk:

Wash my britches
Wash my soul
Here comes a walkin' Tootsie Roll

That song played in my head, 'n' a course it's still there. That song was for all of us who walked. And I told Mom about that this morning, and she said, "Why didn't you tell me about this?" and I said, "Mom, what was the point?" She would have told the principal and then what?

So I use my humor to get through this crap. When you know they don't want you there...I know what my mama was doing was right. [She believed more in her mother being right than in the invective being aimed at her.]

At Little River, where I went to elementary school, when we got new books, we would always be pretty impressed if there were only three names in [the]

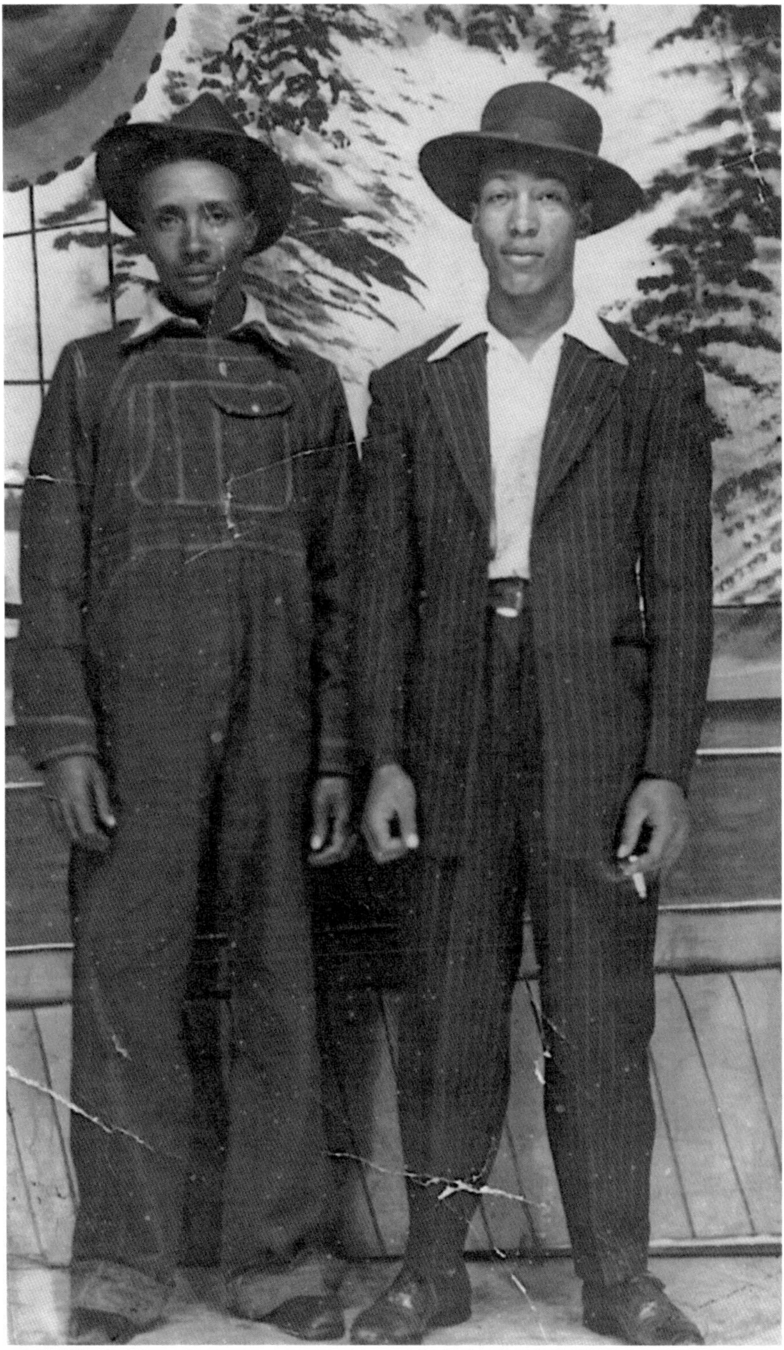

Leroy T. "Hat" Wilson (right) with his friend Mr. Crisp at a fair. *Courtesy of Brenda Stephens.*

book before us because the books we got were the discards from the white schools. We were always behind, and that's what Mama would say. "She's a year behind everybody human; you get out into the world you going to be held back."

"No one's going to invite you to the front of the line," her mother said. "You'll have to push your way up there."

I remember in school later on probably the hardest thing was quantitative physical science. My dad couldn't help with that. He was a farmer. So my mom got a tutor to help. So she's getting up when she should be sleeping to pick me up at school to go to the tutor. So I could see that everything she was doing was for my personal growth.

My grandmother used to say, "Just keep on livin'." I didn't really get that back then but I really get it now. We had to do things a certain way. We had to get up in the morning make our beds—and no snakes in the bed—no sitting on the bed during the day. The bedspread had to be smooth. Beds are for sleeping, chairs are for sitting.

I was in the military—I was only in for a short time, just two years—but long enough to pay for my master's degree. I joined the army, and in basic training, I did great. You don't have to teach me how to make a bed. You don't have to teach me how to clean up.

I had my baby shower at the Confederate Library.

Just before leaving the military, I was approached by the director (of the library) asking if I would be interested in working at the public library—the Confederate Memorial Library. [Asked if she hated saying that word, she said "I do"] I was apprehensive—it was a reduction in salary, there weren't any black people in there. I was the one who was going to make it black.

Stephens was the only person working for the library with a college degree and said her employer was more interested in her race than her qualifications:

Yes, I went to work at the Confederate Memorial Library. There were no black people going into that building. [The Confederate Memorial Library was a whites-only library until Stephens was hired and the county needed to encourage African-American citizens to use the library.] There was another library across town for Negroes. It was the Negro public library. We eventually got some of their books.

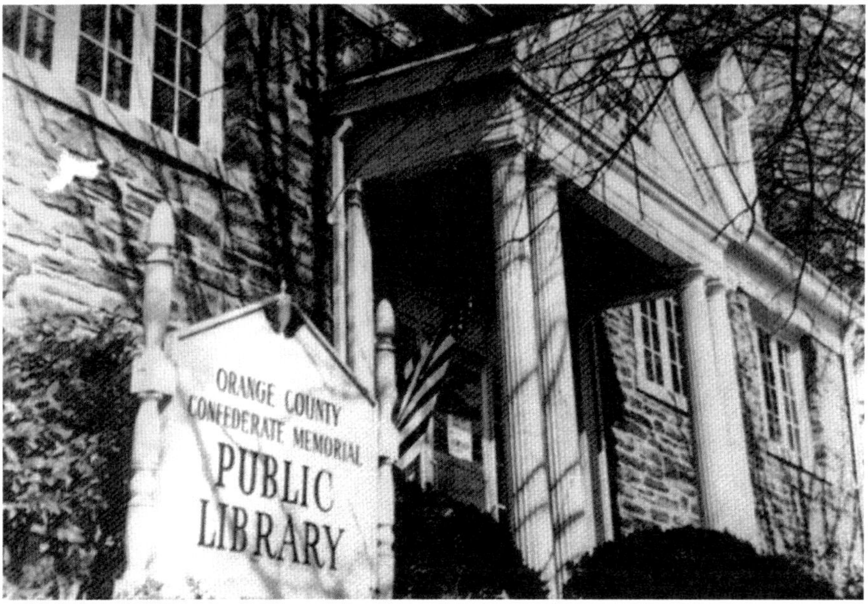

The Orange County Confederate Memorial Public Library. *Courtesy of Brenda Stephens.*

It was a hill to climb, I'll tell you. I used to make trips to the bank for the person in charge and people would stop me. "Do you work in that building? Can we go in that building?" So I guess that's what they wanted. It was working. They weren't going to take out a billboard and say "Come on in, minorities!"

Eventually the commissioners funded the library and removed the name Confederate from the library. I've noticed in stories recently about the history of the library people think that when the library relocated to Tryon Street that that's when it was renamed, but it was actually renamed long before that.

In fact, the word "Confederate" was removed from the original Churton Street building in 2015.

It's amazing [when] I think of it now. People occupied buildings, but they're not identified by the buildings they occupy. I think about that [laughing]. How many kids can say their mom had their baby shower at the Confederate Library?

I started working there in 1976. They wanted me to come to work there, drive the bookmobile, and never asked once if I could drive it. I've never driven a stick in my life. So I got to know the county, got very familiar, got to know a lot of people in the county.

In '77 or '78—and I could do it then because I was young—I had to hold it then for the whole day (my bladder) because I couldn't go in anybody's house. And people would bring me things, they bring food out to the bookmobile but I couldn't go pee in their house. And certain times of the month that was pretty difficult.

It was a mission...so I go home and I say, "Hey, I'm gonna be driving the bookmobile, and I don't know how to drive a stick!" So my daddy said, "I'll teach you this weekend." He had a huge truck, and I drove it up and down the road all weekend. I learned how to back it up, use my mirrors.

That was my first job and that was interesting. It wasn't my background. I have a bachelor's degree in sociology and did my practicum in geriatrics—working with seniors. But I ended up here and you never know what's gonna happen in your life to make a turn. It was not always pleasant.

We've had some brushes with the police...mostly with my black son. I didn't have "the talk" with him. One night we got a call from an officer on Duke's campus and they stopped my son with some [white] girl. He was on a date with his black skin on and driving a foreign car—a BMW that his grandmother had gotten him—and he was detained. So his [white] daddy went over there and cussed them up one side and down the other. The thing was he wasn't doing anything. He was just being black on Duke's campus at night in a foreign car.

One other time at...He was gonna pledge something and he probably did what I did to protect my mama but I think they did something that was going to embarrass him cause I heard about it...but he wouldn't say. I know it was racial. I know it was. Like why you going to stop him for driving that BMW that his grandmama works so hard for? I mean one semester he had to sit out because we couldn't get the money together. So he went to East Carolina.

But Duke is what he wanted and it wasn't always fair. He's told me that he's been watched and followed and that's still going on.

Stevens tells a story of shopping with her husband. He finds some cologne he wants in a display case. They take it out and give it to him for him to purchase it when he's finished shopping. When she chooses some perfume to purchase, the clerk removes it from the display case and says she'll take it to the register for her.

I got a little loud. "Why aren't you taking his?" This crap still happens. This was last year [2014].

When I was working at the Confederate Memorial Library, I got a raise because I've got a master's degree. Somebody working with me said, "What are you going to do with all that money?" And I wondered why? Did I ever ask you what are you going to do with your money?

President Obama's Election

My first reaction to President Obama being elected was fear that somebody's going to kill him. You know when you have somebody who's gonna be a change agent, they want to kill him. And you know my mama would say you have to like the man that respect the position. I know that here in this little library in Hillsborough that a lot of people didn't want to have this colored girl running this library. But he's the president. People should respect the president.

4
NATE DAVIS

Nate Davis was interviewed for the UNC Southern Oral History Program by Bob Gilgor on February 6, 2001, at the Hargraves Community Center in Chapel Hill. The interview's focus began with Lincoln High School (now used by the Chapel Hill Carrboro Schools as a central administration building) but also expanded into larger issues of race.

Well I think, you know, I think I had a pretty good life growing up in the Chapel Hill community, um, I was, I grew up off Church Street on School Lane, between, it was an apartment complex between School Lane and Caldwell Street extension right up from Northside Elementary School. I could look out my bedroom window and see the school, so I didn't have far to walk to school, but it, to me it was a good experience, you know, growing up in that community. I attended Northside Elementary School. We moved from the area probably when I was in the sixth grade.

I grew up with both my parents. My father passed away about five years ago. My father moved here to North Carolina from South Carolina, I think probably in the late '30s, early '40s. My mom is from this area, she was a Trice. She's related to the Markham and Trice families in the Chapel Hill–Carrboro area, so she grew up in this area. They met at Northside Elementary School, which was Orange County Training School at that time and they was married in 1946 or '47.

I have five brothers and four sisters—a real big family. All of them are still in the area, except I have one brother that lives in Chatham County—Siler City—but my other eight brothers and sisters live in this area. I was the third oldest, I had two older brothers. We did have one brother, oldest one, he passed away at birth. Actually not at birth but very young, you know, three or four months old. So he passed away, so it was actually eleven, but I was actually the fourth one out of four boys that was born.

My mom, with that many kids it's kind of hard to get away from the house and work a lot, so my mom stayed at home and raised us. My dad, when we was growing up he worked at the Varsity Theatre as a janitor, and that gave us the opportunity to go and see some of the movies. As you know, back in the early '50s and the '60s and maybe up into the '70s, you know, you were not, African Americans was not allowed to go the movies. So we did have an advantage by going with my dad to work sometimes, to go in and watch some of the movies. I think dad probably worked there until I was about eleven or twelve years old, then he started working at one of the fraternity houses in Chapel Hill, and he worked here until he retired from that, and then he did odd jobs.

My dad was, he was pretty…not sick, but he was sick a lot. He was a diabetic, and I don't remember the exact year, but at some point in time both his legs was amputated because of that, and that's something that runs in my family. But he worked up until the time, probably until the year he passed away, even with both his legs amputated. He worked at the Chapel Hill Tennis Club maintaining the tennis courts for a long time. So yeah, both my parents was around, and my mom, she did do some work every once in a while. She worked at the Carolina Inn as a maid, and you know, odd jobs working in different homes and things like that.

We went with my dad when he went to work and he would turn the movies on. Never attempted to go when the movie was open to the general public, you know—kind of like a private showing. My mom was the boss. She kind of ran things, ran the house, 'cause my dad was away working and things, so my mom would get us up to get ready for school and prepare meals and things like that. We knew all our neighbors. We didn't have that many relatives that lived in the neighborhood where I lived, but you know, back then everyone was kin, you know. It was a duplex and we lived on one side and the Wilsons lived on the other side. Down across the street in front of us Mr. Foushee, Ernest Foushee lived in that apartment. As a matter of fact we stayed in that apartment before we moved across the street to the apartment on School Lane. And then there was Miss Ethel Bynum who lived next door to our duplex and had this beautiful flower garden. All the kids would be outside playing ball and if a ball went in her flower garden, you know, sometimes she would give them back and sometimes she wouldn't. So I do know that Miss Ethel had accumulated a number of softballs and baseballs over the years because they had went into her flower gardens, and so, but we knew everyone that lived in the community, yeah. Where we grew up at it was like a small family because we went to each other's houses and things like that.

There is a ballfield over at Northside. We played on that ballfield. Also there's a little side street which was School Lane, between the houses we played, you know, kickball and things like that, and we had our own bases because there were some rocks, those big old rocks are still there. So those rocks were our bases. Also we played on Caldwell Street—that was the main street. I remember in the summertime a truck would come by to water the road; we would run alongside the truck and get wet and things like that. And also it was an opportunity for us to go into Mr. Wilson Caldwell and Mr. R.D. Smith, and I think Mr. R.D.'s mother lived on the street also. She was a Cub Scout leader, so, but they had the apple trees and pear trees and all that stuff, so we would go and climb the trees and get apples and pears and peaches and things like that.

It was a happy time, you know it was. We went swimming down at the catfish (now Umstead Park). That's where we're still swimming—we had our own swim hole. There was a pool at Umstead, the Exchange Club pool. We were not allowed to go into that pool but you know we had our…We went swimming in the creek. Unfortunately, you know, a lot of us went swimming but I never did learn how to swim that well. But we had fun, we would go down and catch the tadpoles and go swimming and things like that.

We did get in fights, we did. We didn't try to hurt or kill each other back then, but we would um, maybe fight for two or three minutes and then we would go back and play ball. You had people like Miss Ethel Bynum, Mr. Hargraves, Mr. John Bradshaw, Mr. Ernest Foushee. You know, all of them had kids that grew up in that community, so they watched all of us, 'cause from time to time we were at one of their houses playing or eating or sleeping or something.

If there was a problem, you'd get a whipping and then they'd take you home and you'd get another whipping. That's the way it was. How bad? It all depends whether your parents made you go outside and get your own switch, all depends whether you tried to hold the switch and break it, all depends whether you tried to crawl under the bed, and all depends whether you tried to say "Oh mama you done hit me in my eye," or whether—it all depends.

Now if your parents say you go get you a switch so you can get your whipping, and you come back with something small, they may go get something bigger, you know. It was not what people would consider abuse. No, I mean we did get punished. You know we did get punished and you did get your whippings, but it wasn't a beating.

The same in school, if you did something wrong you got the yardstick, you know, you got three or four licks. I think the worst part about it was when you're in the neighborhood, especially in the summertime your doors and windows gonna be open, the worst part about it is trying not to cry because you know everybody's outside listening. And you know, that's when you really got in a fight, after you got a whipping, you know, you're angry and you're upset, but you can't say or do anything to your mom, so you go outside and the guys are gonna get on you so you gonna jump on them, you know, but um, it was not abuse, you know. You didn't talk back. No, you [had] respect for them, they're someone that was not there to harm you, they were people that was there to look out for you and take care of you.

They were there to take care of us. You know, we were like part of their family like I said, back then you know in the neighborhood, the community was just one big family. And you know, our parents knew that they was going to take care of us, you know.

Housing

Okay, we had the kitchen, and then the hallway, and the bathroom, and the bedroom, and then a living room. We had one bedroom up to a point, and then I think the landlord added another bedroom on some years later. But it was not that many kids at that time. Let's see, my brother Bob, my brother Tom, myself, and my sister Willie May, yeah I remember Willie May 'cause she was the baby.

I remember one night myself, Bob and Tom was all in the kitchen area with Willie May, and she was in the baby stroller and we saw this big rat run across the floor, and we all ran out and left her. So there was like four of us back then living in that apartment.

We moved to Merritt Mill Road where the new high school was at that time. We actually purchased a house, my grandparents, they lived there, and they had another house built and we moved in to the house that they lived in. We had two bedrooms then! You know back then everybody had a living room, they had a pull-out couch, and so some people did sleep on the pull-out couch, so we had three bedrooms.

I'm trying to think, my brother, I think my sister Helen and my brother Kenny may have been born later on when we moved to Rangewood, out on 54 West where my mother lives now, but it was at least eight. We didn't feel poor. We were, but we didn't feel it, because we had all the love. We had people in the community like Mr. Bynum Weaver that looked after us, you know that provided different things that people needed in the community that couldn't afford to buy, you know, as far as wood, kerosene for the stove, food.

There was some people, especially Mr. Bynum Weaver and Susie Weaver, you know, he gave everything. I think no one would, everyone knew that he gave to people but I don't think no one would ever really realize how much he did give. He was owner of a little convenience store down on Brooks Street and also he owned the funeral home in Chapel Hill. Miss Susie was in the funeral business with him and she also had a radio program, a gospel program on Sundays, and I think she was a beautician. I think she was a beautician and also worked at the funeral home. Mr. Bynum owned it. It was the Bynum Weaver Funeral Home.

Oh yeah, back then you took care of each other, you know, you took care of your family. And family back then didn't necessarily have to mean that you were blood kin. You know, someone you knew, someone you cared for, someone in the community, you know, that was family.

Back then everybody went to church. But yeah, we didn't feel poor. People may have looked at certain people and said well they're poor, they don't have. I think some people felt like that they was a little bit better or had more than other people, you know.

Family and Education

My grandmom was a wonderful lady. She was the backbone of the family now. I think especially for my mom and my dad, they taught us to be honest, not to lie, cheat or steal, um, to be honest and to be who you are. To not try to pretend to be more than you are. And to love and to share. My grandma, you know, could take care of yourself.

When we moved down to on Merritt Mill Road, our house was here and then on the other side was my grandma's house and on the other side was my uncle, my grandma's brother. Across the street was my granddad's brother, then further down was my mother's parents, my other grandparents, so when we moved out Merritt Mill Road, it was a big community but I had more relatives that lived down in that area, on Merritt Mill Road.

Education was very important. Very important, you know. I think everybody in the community made it important. My father did not graduate from high school, I forget how far he went in school. But my mom graduated. As a matter of fact, she graduated top in her class. She didn't continue her education, because she got married, you know. All except two of my siblings graduated high school. My sister Helen who is a schoolteacher now [went to college]. She graduated, my brother Ollie, N.T., I attended North Carolina Central University, let's see…yeah, about four of us. You know all of them has good jobs, you know jobs good enough to support them and everything. We had books, because you know, I spent some time back and forth, you know, my house and my grandma's house, and all of my grandma's kids except for my dad graduated from high school, and they had material around. They left, went up north, so there was stuff left there, you know, for us. I think we had a good childhood. We didn't have everything that other people may have had, you know and things like that, but I think basically it was, I wouldn't say rough, you know it was difficult, we didn't have everything that we wanted or needed, you know. But we got things, you know, from time to time.

In 1962, I went to Chapel Hill Junior High School up on Franklin Street. It was a choice, I think it was a choice that certain people in the community and your parents made. In a way I wanted to, because I got bribed by my grandparents [laughter]. You know, back then some people thought this was a wonderful thing, and they, you know, some parents really felt proud that their child or grandchild was going to be a part of this. I recall Miss Gloria Williams who was a big part of this community, who passed away about a year ago, I think she was a part of it.

Desegregation

I think before that some had gone to the elementary school. I don't know when Stanley Vickers went, it may have been three years before then, but maybe Stanley Vickers and a few other ones. Myself, Keith Edwards, David Briggs, Pernell Jackson, James Britt, I do remember those five. There may have been some that didn't hang with us, but I do remember those five—Carrie, Keith, James, Pernell, David Briggs and myself.

I don't remember that first day for some reason. I know I used to sit in class and cry a lot. I was afraid of what was going to happen once I walked out of the classroom. We were called names, some people wanted to fight, you know. It lasted most of that year—seventh grade year and then the following year at Guy B. Phillips and a lot of it continued. As a matter of fact it was to the point where it was so bad my first year at Guy B. Phillips—no one was aware of it and no one probably cared, you know with the school system—I played hooky. Not every day, but for about two or three months I stayed out of school. And you know, I just didn't go. And no one missed me and no one cared, you know. But then more people started coming to the junior high school and it got a little bit better, we had more teachers that cared about us, and kind of looked after us.

If I'd played hooky from Northside, the teacher would leave the classroom and walk across the field, or go to your house, get in their car and go to your house and see what was wrong, you know. School was fun back then. You had a good time. I'm pretty sure there's still some things that are still being said. People may not be using the same language, and you know, but I'm pretty sure that some things are still being said about different races, whether it's white or black, you know. I'm not saying that all the whites and all the teachers were like that. We had some, I think one thing that helped me survive up on Franklin Street at Chapel Hill Junior High School was some of the white friends we had, male and female. You know, I remember I used to be sitting there in class, be crying and, you know, and I don't remember the name, there were these two white girls that used to just talk to me, and this was mainly in my math class. And I think the main reason I cried in that class was because I had just left my history class and we had a very, very mean history teacher and she wouldn't say "Negro," she said "niggras."

There were fights, but like I said I had this real close friend, a guy named Reedy Hilton. His father was the track coach at Carolina for a long time. I think Reed still lives here in Chapel Hill—lives out in Chatham County now. He was a close friend and he would always stop us from fighting. He was a white student. And this other guy named Kenny Rogers—I don't know where Kenny's at now—Kenny used to be a Chapel Hill police officer here in Chapel Hill, and I haven't seen him in a while, but you'd have people like that that would kind of intervene, and help out.

I was an athlete, so kind of, you know, if you were an athlete you had a little bit of advantage. I didn't play much sports in junior high school up on Franklin Street, but once I got out to Guy B. Phillips I played basketball, ran track. I think it helped, but it didn't help overall because when you went to another school to play and sometimes being the only black athlete out there on the basketball court, you get called all kind of names. I think it had a real lasting effect on me because after that I was always nervous when I went out on the court, you know to play football, basketball, something like that. It didn't bother me when I was running track, but other sports it did, and it followed me through high school, and I was always nervous when I went out there. This taunting stayed with me until I stopped playing sports. I think you get over it by protecting the ones you love and making sure that's not going to happen to them. That's where I get over it.

And it didn't just happen in the schools, it was in the community back then. So you know, a lot of people look at integration and say the blacks had all these problems, but you know, we had those problems before we went into the school system. When you left Lincoln you had problems. When you left your community you had problems. When we left Merritt Mill Road, when we left Northside area, and went downtown into the community, you had those problems. So it was just not in the school system.

I think back then the parents, you know, wanted us to stay in our place, you know, stay in your community. I remember because you had the junior high school here, then you had the high school and it was separated by an auditorium. Then you had (in the back) was the arts and crafts building, and then you had the gymnasium and the P.E. department was kind of in the back. We came out the door from the junior high school, myself and David Briggs and Pernell Jackson, we would walk across the street to the Exxon service station which is now McFarling's Exxon, we would walk down the street past where BW3 is now, used to be the old Belk's and feed store. We'd cross over to go to the gymnasium and to go to the arts and crafts building because we didn't want to walk behind the school.

There was a fraternity house and sometimes the students from the fraternity house would come over there and bother us, not just us but all the students. So we would walk across the street and go down and come back across to get to class so we wouldn't have to go through the back where everybody would be. There was a snack bar back there so all the students would be back there, you know.

Miss Zora Rashkis cared about everybody. She cared about everybody, she wanted to make sure that everybody succeeded. We had this black girl that was in my class, and um, she was always late, two or three minutes, whatever, five minutes. And Miss Rashkis kept telling her, you know, you need to get to class on time, and she said I can't do it, I can't do it. And she explained to her why she could not get there on time. And one day Miss Rashkis said, well, that's it, you have to be in class on time. The very next day she was in class on time. Miss Rashkis told her, okay, I understand why you were being late, now we can deal with that, we can work with that, you can be late. But I want you to try to get here on time. But I just wanted to show you that you could get here on time. You know, Zora Rashkis taught values. She taught you, um, she made you feel a part of everybody. She wanted you to understand and to know that you could be just as important as the next person regardless of whether you're white or black. She opened her home up to all the students in her class, and she wanted you to know that you could succeed, you could do things. Just like the young lady that kept coming to class late, you know, she wanted her to prove to herself that she could be on time. I think Miss Rashkis probably invited everybody into her home.

I got an education. That's one good thing that came out of it. I did get an education, and whether it was the best education a black student could have received at that time is debatable. I think it did hurt in a way because you was in an environment that you didn't want to be in, an environment where you couldn't really concentrate on what you was doing, concentrate on your work, because you had so many other things that would draw your attention away – whether it was that you didn't have money to do this, or you were afraid what was going to happen when you went to another class or left school that day or came to school the next day. So you did get an education, but you know, there were some stumbling blocks and some things in your way that would not have been in your way if you was at Lincoln, you know.

It was a different environment. At Northside Elementary School you had a closer relationship, you knew the teacher, you felt comfortable. And you know all the students in class, so you had people to work with, people to help you out if you had a problem. And in junior high school it was more like you were on your own, you know. But you know, like I say, and I really hate to start calling names because there was a lot of good teachers, you know Miss Rashkis, Zora Rashkis, and Miss Stanford, really sticks out and there was a history teacher by the name of Mr. Vaughn I think and people like that.

This history teacher, I had her in the seventh grade and I said, God, I done got rid of her when I left Chapel Hill Junior High School and went to Guy B. Phillips, but I got her again out there in eighth grade. We was in class one day, and this was when President Kennedy was assassinated. And she made a statement, she said "I bet some niggra did it," you know, right in class.

Then I went to the new Chapel Hill High School, there was like a lapse, because the year that I played hooky for so long, I didn't pass my grade that year, because I just didn't do nothing. And I kind of like hung out in the woods. And um, and I think, one day, when you hung out in the woods you hung out near Lincoln, because you wanted to see everything that was going on. You wanted to see all the activities they was doing, like the May Day program, and the different activities they had, and the band practicing and the football team practicing, and you know, the students and people going to lunch and stuff like that. Everybody wanted to be a part of that. I think every black child in Chapel Hill grew up wanting to be a part of Lincoln High School. And they knew if you went to Lincoln High School you had to do what was right, because Mr. McDougle would not have it any other way. You know, he was the principal, and he would come by your house, you know, he would be driving down the street and he may see five of us, you know, some guys out in the yard, and he would stop by your house and talk to you, whether it was in the afternoon, or Saturday, or Sunday, or whatever.

Everybody called him McDougle. He would stop and come to your house and get on you and talk to you, and talk to your parents, and everything, even if you were not a student at Lincoln. But everybody wanted to go to Lincoln, but when they built Chapel Hill High School (when it first opened) I went to Chapel Hill High School. We knew (it would be integrated). A lot of people was hoping—myself for one—that that was the year that we were going to be able to go back to Lincoln, because everybody grew up wanting to play sports at Lincoln. I used to get up and you know, the football and basketball games, which I could walk to the gym, but on Saturday mornings when my two brothers would go play baseball and run track, you know the bus would come by the house and pick them up, and I'm sitting there wanting to go, couldn't go. Everybody grew up wanting to go to Lincoln, to be a part of that program. Whether the band, the drill team, the basketball team, the football team, or whatever. Everybody, every black child grew up wanting to be a part of Lincoln High School. And there was so much there, I mean, everything, you know, I mean it was so much we saw growing up. You probably had more people at practice than at games sometimes because everybody wanted to go see Lincoln. That's the way it was.

You had more blacks out there (my first year in high school). As we looked at it, you had the guys from Lincoln that came, so we felt like then that, hey, we got our protection out here. You know, you had the people like Thurman Couch, Rudolph Farrell, Charles Farrington, Larry, it was Henry Campbell, Henry McCray, you had all those guys and more that was coming out there. And these were like the big, which there was only like a year apart in our age.

Well some of that had kind of gone away, because my ninth grade year at Phillips I played basketball. So since I played basketball I kind of you know had more friends, um, but I do recall going back a little bit, one day at basketball practice, myself and there was two other guys, Jesse Chavis and another guy, was on the JV basketball team out there, and some of the guys said let's go to the store, you know, and we were going to walk from Phillips down to the bottom of the hill, where the Texaco service station is now. There used to be a little store there—Brady's. So on the way down the street, these guys kept whispering at each other. Billy Andrews and a guy named Bobby who was

Coach Carleton's son, who was a high school coach, and Jimmy Vann and all those guys, you know, they kept whispering to each other, and I'm trying to figure out, what are they…what's going on? I didn't know.

We get to the store, and one of the guys says "Well Nate, let me have your money." And I should have known, but you know, I had…some time…you know back then some of us kind of got in a position where we kind of forgot you know where we had come from and everything. I think that at one point in time I'm out there playing basketball with them, I'm a basketball star, and what they do I can do. On this particular day thought that I could walk with them to the store and go into the store, you know. And I couldn't go in. This was my ninth grade year, so this was like '65.

You might have had the federal civil rights law, but there still was some people that would tell you that you couldn't come into the store. And I'm, you know, I don't know the owner of the store but the little store on the corner, I don't think it was Brady's restaurant then. It was like a candy store or soda store. So they said well give me your money and we'll bring you something back out. I said "Well what's going on?" They said "Well you can't go in with us." So I turned around and walked on back on up the hill to the school and they went in the store.

CHAPEL HILL HIGH SCHOOL

With the teachers, they brought some of the black teachers out, you know, Mr. McDougle came, Mr. R.D. Smith, so we had some people that we could go to, people that we could talk to if we had a problem. People that was out there that was going to make sure that we got a good education and we was treated fairly. So we had people like that. You had Coach Culton who was the football, basketball, track, swim, golf, he coached everything. He was there and kind of took care of student athletes. And Coach Peerman was out there also. He was assistant coach, he was JV coach. I played JV football, so I got the opportunity to play under him. He was a good coach, he was a good person, you know, a good role model, he looked out for everyone. He was a fair coach, whether you was white or black. With all the blacks that came out to Chapel Hill High School back then, I think they kind of felt like that they was gonna be mistreated. Like Mr. McDougle, he was assistant principal, I think he was in charge of books.

This community knew that all the black teachers at Lincoln was not going to be brought out to Chapel Hill High School. Lincoln stayed open for a while as a school as like an elementary and middle school, so there was still some classes at Lincoln and some of the teachers stayed down there.

In 1968, tensions were increasing at Chapel Hill High School. Other former students interviewed for the Southern Oral History Project confirm what Nate Davis remembers about what some referred to as a "riot" and by most reasonable standards would be best described as an outburst. Walter Durham said, "This was just a bunch of unruly teenagers with no direction. We didn't march off campus but I guess that's the one thing that didn't cause us to get what we were after because there really wasn't no structure in it. It really wasn't organized."

The event itself consisted of a few African-American students chaining and locking some doors and declaring themselves in control. They felt they were being controlled and thought they would return the favor to make a point. There were no arrests. There was no damage to the school. Many of these students, according to Durham, just wanted to back to the family atmosphere at Lincoln High School. Nate Davis, like many of his classmates, seemed to feel torn.

I don't remember a lot about the riot. I think the black students wanted to be a part, they wanted to be heard, to let people know that they were part of the school. And I think the main thing, they wanted it to be their school also. You know, I can remember the first year in '66, we had an excellent football team. We went to Roxboro, and played Roxboro and they beat us. They beat us. They really beat us.

The next week at practice, Coach Culton walked out on the field, and he was real quiet, you know. He had this letter in his hand. Somebody at Roxboro had wrote him a letter and this is what it was saying, "Do not never bring those niggers up here to try to beat us in football again." So, things like that happened. We would go places and play games. There were some teams that still didn't have any blacks on their teams, so we encountered a lot of hatred from that. I think it just kind of carried over and what had happened, you had basically taken something from both races. You had the white race that felt like Chapel Hill High is our school, you know, and you had the black race saying well, Lincoln High was our school. So you took Lincoln from them and you also took Chapel Hill High from the whites. Because they grew up saying "This is my school." And we grew up saying "Lincoln and Northside is our school." I feel like you just didn't take something from the blacks, but you also took something from the whites, also. You probably had a lot of hatred and a lot of hostility and anger built up in both races.

I would go as far as to say, if we ran into any type of hostility, racism from another school, I would say you had the support of most if not all of the football members. You know, Chapel Hill was a small place. And a lot of people grew up in Carrboro and Chapel Hill. So we knew some of the people that we went to school with and played football with, and it was not like, every day someone was running around calling us niggers and stuff like that. It's not like we couldn't sit down beside him, or when we walked into the shower everybody, all the whites would walk out…it was not like that.

The Death of Martin Luther King Jr.

I think you probably had a lot of white students that was afraid, you had black students that was angry. No one knew what was going to happen. You probably had some white students that was trying to get across to their black friends, yes, this did happen but I'm not a part of it; you know me, you know who I am, you know what I believe in—I've been your friend. I think there would have been less racism coming from the white students if it was not for some of their parents. A lot of the students that we had problems with, or that I have a problem with now, or back then, are my friends, I would consider them friends. Someone I have sat down and had lunch with or whatever, that I see in the community and things like that…I think that it was something that they grew up with. It was something that was taught. And it took them a time to learn that this is not the way it should be, this is not the way I want to be.

That was something that was never discussed—how to treat whites. We knew that if you went certain places you would be discriminated against, but as far as your parents telling you, well don't trust this white person because they're going to do this to you…it was not the person but the situation you were put in—where you went, how you handled yourself when you went certain places. We had everything we needed in our community, so we really didn't have to go anywhere, you know. We had our school, we had our churches. I was not lucky enough to be old enough to go to the movie theater that used to be up here in Carrboro, but you know, back then they had the movie theater, and we had Hargraves. Hey, you got everything you needed at Hargraves. I been coming to Hargraves since I was five years old.

I have a seventeen-year-old, a twenty-six-year-old and a twenty-four-year-old son that graduated from Chapel Hill High. I don't hear so much about race relations, you know, as with any institution these days they are good and positive. My son is a pretty good student, he's an athlete, so he may not

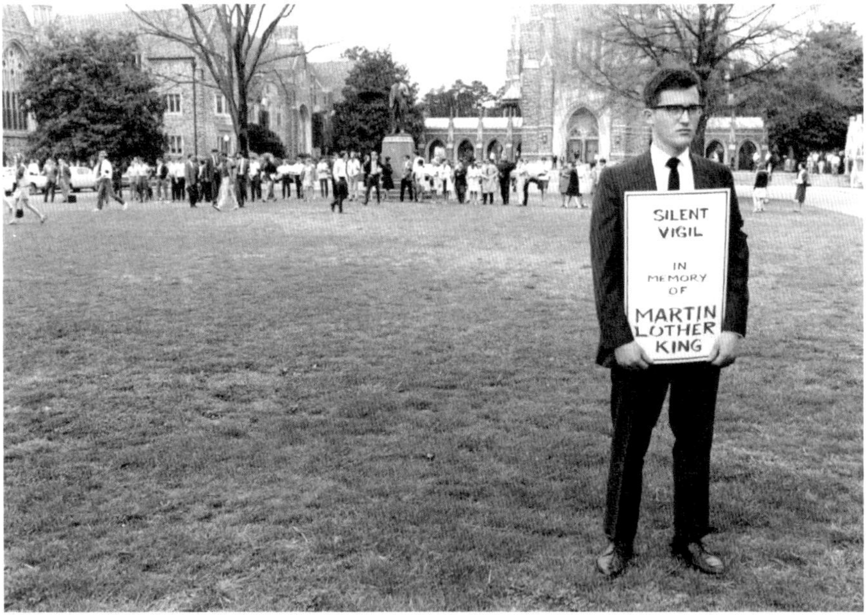

A Duke student participates in a silent protest following the death of Martin Luther King Jr. in April 1968. *Photograph by Bill Boyarsky, courtesy of the Durham County Library Collection.*

encounter some of the things that the other black kids may encounter. And also with Chapel Hill, some people may deny this and say it's not true, but it's who you are and that's the way it is.

It all depends on how you were treated. The person that's treated with respect, all depends on who you got, who's got your back and that's the bottom line. You know, if you may have a student out there that may have one parent in the home and the mother's working three or four jobs, but if the community is behind you, you're not going to have too much of a problem. If you're mistreated in this community, if the powers that be know that you may have someone that's going to look out for you, they kind of lay off you a little bit more. I'm not saying that you get away with doing anything wrong. Like when I was growing up, well and I'm not that much younger than Fred, but you know, you had people like Fred Ballard and Hank Anderson, Hilliard Caldwell and people like that and there's others out there that's going to take care of you.

We came to Hargraves and our parents had come to Hargraves, we didn't have nothing to worry about. They knew where we was at. Miss Lucille Caldwell was here when you was at Hargraves. And there was a certain time she was going to send you home when you was supposed to be home. They knew what you were going to get into over here. I'm not saying that's a good thing or a bad thing, because I think there's certain people in this community that look out for all the young people. As for myself, if you want to, if you really want to get my dander and get me angry, mistreat a young person. And I still have to catch myself sometimes from getting too angry. Like some people may say something like, "those people" that live in public housing, or "those people," or "that child," you know. And I really get angry when people say that, regardless of who it is. Because they're labeling those people, and to me, it makes me feel like that they feel like they're better than they are.

One thing about Hargraves, if you come here, you can be treated the same way, regardless of who you are. I think some kids kind of take advantage of that when they come over here, because they may do something and it may seem that I'm getting angry and they'll stand there and look at me and say well, he's not going to make us leave. Let's just go stand around the back of the building about five or ten minutes and then he's going to come looking for us. But this is a place for them to come and have fun and be protected. There's a lot of people in this community that take care of the young people in this community and the same thing with the school system. You have to go there and be an advocate for them, speak out for them and make sure they're not being mistreated. It just all depends on who you are and what you're doing and who you know. I reckon it's the same way everywhere, with just about everything.

5

JAKI SHELTON GREEN

We are a family that has persevered from fields to classrooms, higher education, PhDs, board rooms, courtrooms.

Jaki Shelton Green is the author of Dead on Arrival, Dead on Arrival and New Poems, Masks, Conjure Blues, Singing a Tree Into Dance, Breath of the Song, Blue Opal *(a play) and* Feeding the Light *(published by Jacar Press). She is the coeditor of two anthologies:* Immigration Emigration *and* Diversity and Poets for Peace *published by Chapel Hill Press.*

Her numerous honors as a North Carolina writer are best summed up by one of her latest recognitions—her 2014 induction into the North Carolina Literary Hall of Fame. Born in 1953, she came of age during the civil rights struggle and has played a continual role in telling her own truth about rights and violence and kindness and love. Fortunately for the larger community, she also makes a great deal of investment in teaching others to do the same.

My parents, Carnish Vincent and Ivory Tate Vincent, raised me and my brother, Jerald, in Efland, North Carolina, the "home-place" for my mother's patrilineal and matrilineal lineage. My father grew up in Greensboro and my mother grew up in Efland. After returning from the army, my father continued in the footsteps of his father, working for different mortuary businesses until he was disabled in the early 1960s due to a series of strokes and heart attacks. He eventually suffered a major heart attack and died in 1970. My mother was my father's care-provider while simultaneously maintaining a household, working a series of jobs (laundry services, domestic, nanny, community agency field supervisor,

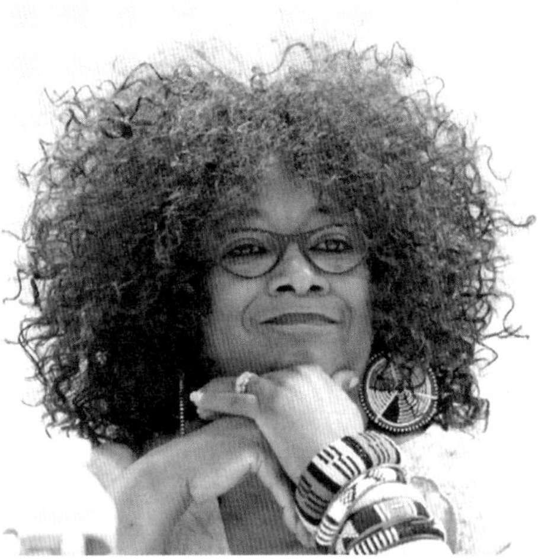

North Carolina Literary Hall of Fame poet Jaki Shelton Green. *Photograph by Sylvia Freeman.*

industrial plants, Health Education and Welfare (HEW) program assistant) in order to provide for our family. There were no public benefits or assistance. Our family relied on the self-sufficiency of my mother and the generosities of our supportive family circle.

The family clan I grew up within included my maternal grandmother, my mother's siblings and their families. My aunts were teachers. One uncle was a principal, and two uncles were successful businessmen. I grew up understanding and appreciating what it meant to be self-reliant and the merits of social entrepreneurship. The models were demonstrative in an extended-family unit that shared a family garden providing much of the food we consumed.

My uncle Ervin made long trips "Down-East" and returned with produce that he sold. His thriving service station–general store served the community. My uncle Nathaniel was a store owner and successful tailor. I learned as a child how to "run the stores with Grandma" and the importance of customer service, gratitude and the spirit of generosity. I was influenced by the people who came from all over, bringing their lore to my uncle's store. I knew about the Green Book because my uncle gave them away to black motorists who stopped for a pit stop, gas and a Coca-Cola on their journeys farther South. White businessmen, salesmen and politicians especially loved to drop by pushing their cheap wares or begging for the "colored vote."

My brother and I are the youngest of five grandchildren on my mom's side of the family. I was infatuated with my two older female cousins. The way they dressed, their hairstyles, their confidence as older more sophisticated young ladies was poetry in itself. The women in my family love beautiful men, beautiful homes, beautiful clothes, beautiful jewelry, beautiful yards and good food. My grandmother was a quilter who wove not just haberdashery scraps into quilts but she also wove jewel-toned silks, brocades, crêpe de chine, Chantilly lace, delicate linens and cashmere remnants of ball gowns, prom dresses, Easter dresses, wedding dresses of daughters and granddaughters. Inside each stitch was a family story such as the quilts she created for us as young children from the pajamas, smocked dresses, plaid tartan skirts and pants that we grew out of. Meals and the presentation of food taught me the fine art of sensuality and an appreciation for the healing and nurturing powers of culinary finesse.

This sweet family that I was born into taught me that perhaps the most important and simplest gift to each other is maintaining strong family narratives. We have many, as well as the many rituals and traditions we hold dear, but we have no myths. My family honors and passes down the histories and herstories of grandparents, great-grandparent and ancestors. My brother and I, along with our cousins, know where our parents went to school, who their childhood friends were and the memorable milestones of their lives. These stories have been told over and over again…and now our children and grandchildren know the source of where our stories begin. Like us, our children will know the names of the ones who came before us; we bear their likenesses…the lineage who endured slavery, Jim Crow and strode in freedom. They will know the places they worked and where they are buried. As a family, we all know the stories of our individual births, and we continue to tell our offspring the stories of their own unique births. We are a family that has persevered from fields to classrooms, higher education, PhDs, board rooms, courtrooms. These are rich stories told during my childhood and my children's childhoods on porches, church pews, around dining tables, while fishing or in gardens.

My voice as a writer was unconsciously taking form as I listened to descriptive and lyrical stories that stretched beyond my family circle into the homes of neighbors, relatives and people who helped to shape my lens of what it means "to utter; to tell." I found the essence of story-creating, refining, retelling…listening to the many voices of family and community. Those "found stories" shaped my own interior voice and helped me extract the exterior of landscape and physicality that informs how my writing becomes a vessel where the stories can thrive for many generations to come.

My childhood in Efland was in a safe, nurturing community anchored by faith, family connections and a deep sense of communal goodwill. I attended segregated public schools (first through ninth grade) in Orange County, attended OHS my sophomore year and enrolled for junior and senior high school years at a private Quaker boarding school in Bucks County, Pennsylvania. I am forever grateful for the mean-spiritedness that was rampant during the desegregation of Orange County schools. I was kicked out of OHS for my civil disobedience of participating in a school "walkout." That denial and mistreatment served me well as I was welcomed into a very different environment that encouraged the questioning of ethical and moral behaviors and the right to exercise free speech. During this period of personal and social unrest coupled with the usual stresses of adolescence, I began writing with a fervor. Since [I was] six, my mother had given my diaries. These journals became more and more important as I wrote about the changing world of the South I knew and how my new experiences with diversity on so many levels were informing and shaping my political, social and cultural perspectives.

The George School was the beginning of a new way of "being" in life that provided rich instruction for college, graduate school, raising a family and my emergence as a published writer. Through it all, though, it is the presence of childhood friends who are still present that help to ground my presence in the world. We navigated the same waters of coming to age in a small, rural community. We lifted each other's self-esteem. We learned our first lessons in trust from each other. The friendship habits I created as a child continue to hold me close to many childhood pals. Childhood friendships hold all the stories of good and bad experiences—from ridiculous hairstyles, clothing choices, to questionable relationships. Old friends hold the empathy for us and whole space with us in sorrow and in celebration. These unique friends have pushed me beyond comfort zones encouraging me to do things I might not have done. My old friends know my family, know my mama's cobbler and my aunt's potato salad. They "know things." They are "my people." There is a different kind of kinship in friendship that forms from navigating growing up. Sense of place and sharing a unique hometown culture is the strong emphasis that bonds us and keeps these friendships alive. Those kinships from home were the foundation that helped me to understand how to form strong relationships in new places. My intimate teenage George School friendships run deep and also remain strong anchors in my life.

My family was strong politically. I remember the March on Washington as a child, the assassinations of MLK, Malcolm X, John and Robert Kennedy and the civil rights movement.

I heard the speeches, read the poetry and witnessed the artistry emerge up front and personal as America, too, was being stretched racially and politically. I was hungry for new knowledge, ripe for a reeducation. I read Kwame Nkrumah, Sonia Sanchez, Gwendolyn Brooks, Malcolm X, Franz Fanon, Eldridge Cleaver, Amiri Baraka. I listened to the Last Poets, John Coltrane, Abbey Lincoln, Yusef Lateef, Nina Simone, Pharoah Sanders, Joan Baez, Laura Nyro. I attended marches, speeches, Black Panther rallies, Pan African meetings. All of these experiences helped me understand the role and stances my family upheld in the struggles for equality, human and civil rights, and the importance of the *vote.* I witnessed my mother and other relatives investing long hours registering people to vote, driving people to polls, encouraging people to become very knowledgeable about the political arena and how it impacted our quality of life. I have followed suit as a political and cultural activist.

Standing, voting for the first time was overwhelming and powerful because I invited all of my ancestors, especially, the unnamed ones whose bones are buried at the bottom of the Atlantic to come hold space with me, help me lift the pen, help me mark the X. I invited them again to hold the pen and make my X when I voted for Barack Obama. These ancestors provided the necessary strength that is in our collective DNA; a strength that helped us all vote this young lion of African descent into the White House and into a deeper reality of an America that continues to deny us the vestiges of being human.

I have been writing since childhood. I have experienced many transitions in my personal and professional life that have shifted how my voice shows up, but my voice remains the same...decidedly female, seeped in oral traditions, history/herstory. Writing is a powerful tool for transformation, for healing, for building communities. My poems are embedded in story.

I asked Shelton Green which writers have influenced her. It is quite a list:

Phillis Wheatley
Mari Evans
Pablo Neruda
Rumi
Hafiz
Grimm's fairy tales
Shakespeare
Lucille Clifton
Audre Lorde
Sonia Sanchez
Robert Hayden
Alice Walker
Sylvia Plath
Anne Sexton
Amiri Baraka
Isabelle Allende
Paulo Coelho
Deena Metzger
Tempest Williams
Carolyn Forché
Lidia Yuknavitch
Mary Oliver

Traveling the world listening, telling, and gathering has intensified my commitment to continue to use poetry/story-telling as the archetype of the bridge that connects our sameness...we have different tongues, different skins, but the essence of the story is a river where all our blood is born. So we tell... so the ones after us will continue to tell.

6

JACKIE WAGSTAFF

Basically people want fair and decent housing. They want jobs that provide decent income. They want safe neighborhoods for their kids to grow up. They want decent education.

Jacqueline "Jackie" Denise Wagstaff represents an important transition in Durham's civil rights history. She was interviewed on December 1, 1998, by Alicia Rouverol for the University of North Carolina's Southern Oral History Program. Her story ranges from being a community organizer to a fall from grace and influence into disrepute, disruption and frustration, much of which occurred after this interview took place.

Wagstaff's story reveals a surprising thread that starts with the loss of her mother when Wagstaff was a young child and her sense of disconnection as a result. Her work as an activist in Durham's schools, organizing low-income families to benefit from their collective strength in numbers, was often confrontational and disruptive.

After this interview took place, Wagstaff's activism was expressed through her leadership position in the Durham Committee (on the Affairs of Black People). Always a lightning rod, Wagstaff's tactics eventually went too far, members felt. The time for interrupting and disrupting was over, the group determined. In local politics, the Durham Committee determined it was ready to close that chapter in its history. They wanted to engage more community members to join their cause and felt that Wagstaff's methods were keeping people away.

In the summer of 2013, an emergency meeting of the group's executive committee voted to remove Wagstaff from leadership. According to news reports, North Carolina senator

Floyd McKissick Jr. was appointed to temporarily take her place as chair of the group's policial committee, whose responsibilities included interviewing local election candidates for the purposes of issuing endorsements. It sent a shock wave through the local political scene. Wagstaff still had many outspoken supporters who complained about the ouster. Her long service to the Durham Committee was respectfully acknowledged by allowing her to serve out her term as chair, but the committee was moving on.

In a subsequent meeting, Walter Jackson took over that role. At least between the covers of this book, it is a small world.

Family

Most of my aunts and uncles and cousins still live in New Rochelle. So most of my family—most of my family is in New Rochelle, and D.C. and Maryland. I have an uncle and an aunt that lives in Sedalia and one lives still in Caswell County. That's it.

Being raised in North Carolina after my mother died. That's the connection to North Carolina. Being in Caswell County, like I said, grew up in a rural area. And kind of went to school in a rural area, did rural things. That's where my roots are. That's where I consider my roots are in North Carolina. New Rochelle is my birthplace but my roots are in North Carolina. I was four going on five. I had two brothers. Actually, my youngest brother was already here. My oldest brother, he and I, remained in New York until Uncle Martin decided if we'd be best if we were raised in the country. So that's how we ended up here.

My mom died when I was four. I never really got to know her. I just kind of hear things and…pictures and stuff like that. I never really got to know her. So that's probably a part of me that I guess my drive to help other people and relate to their families because of that fact. Sometimes you miss that part. It's not the same being raised by somebody else. It's okay. But it's not the same. Because my aunt and uncle, they were real strict. It was very structured and very strict. I'm not going to say it was the best environment but we didn't go without. They never had kids of their own. So we were their kids. But at the same time that's another difference. Unless you have kids, I think there's something missing. I think it's more of an adjustment.

When you have your own kids it's not so much of an adjustment. This is my extended family. But to actually take on someone else's kids and you don't have any kids and never had experience with any kids. I'm given a family and I have to adjust to it. So it was kind of like that. I had two brothers. I have an older brother and a younger brother. When my mother died, my youngest brother was only about six months old. He actually spent all of his life with my aunt and uncle because they got him from the time that he was six months old. When my mother died we actually spent like another year or two in New Rochelle before we actually transitioned here. It worked out. It just wasn't the same as being raised by your parents, your real parents.

The land was passed down from my grandfather. It's about a hundred acres. My mother's share was passed down to my brother and myself. So we have her land. Basically we just kind of farmed the land because all of my aunts and uncles—they never made a life in North Carolina. After they grew up and came of age they left North Carolina (most of them) migrated to New York. That's how they ended up in New York. They decided they didn't want to be farmers. So all of my aunts and uncles left and moved away. And my one uncle he stayed and he farmed the land. He kept the land, paid taxes on it and everything. That's why the land stays in the family. He bought other land. As we grew up it was like he bought other farms and other land. So we have a lot of land in Caswell County.

It was structured, very structured, because they was like strict. And they had certain beliefs. A lot of times a lot of my belief plays into what I do. Growing up a certain way it wasn't like growing up in the city. It was just certain things that I believe in and certain things that I do. It was hard. It was hard work. I'm not going to say it wasn't hard work. Because you had to do things like you had to get up before daybreak, milk a cow, feed pigs, do whatever you had to do. And that was before you went to school.

We still went to school. You get on a bus and you ride about an hour or two because the nearest school was in Yanceyville. So we had to ride for about an hour or two to get to school. So it was kind of nontraditional but at the same time you had value. That's some of the values that I grew up with. They were traditional Baptists, very traditional Baptists. They believed that we had to believe the same thing that they believed. Now I'm traditional Baptist. I believe I'm very spiritual, but I would never impose on my children what they imposed on us when it came to religion. I gave my children the opportunity to decide what they want to believe. I provide the core but they basically make the decision on what they want to believe. I'm not going to push it down their throat.

At the same time, there are things like, I believe that Sunday morning I want to get up and go to Sunday school. I don't care where you go. Right now we attend First Baptist, which is a white church. But it's Baptist. It's not traditional in the sense of what I grew up with, but it's traditional in the sense of what I want to be involved with now. What I grew up with would be basically your basic small congregational church. You had traditional people. You had people that were in charge of certain things. Everything was structured. You have your minister that did this. You had your congregation, your deacons, your sisters and all of this that did certain things in the church. My uncle was one of those important people in the church. He managed the finances. He managed the books. He was one of those people that were very important, key to the church and we had to follow suit because he did hold that position in church.

I had to do certain things that I really didn't want to do sometimes. But had to do them because they said that's what you had to do. Like go represent the church when you had to go to big conferences. We had these things called associations. Where all of the different churches come together and you had to have representation. You had people that when they call your church name, somebody had to get up and do something to represent the church. I always got stuck with it. I'd be so nervous, I mean, I just was not going to do it. And I just hated it. And I was always pushed into doing it, things like ushering in church on Sunday, you had to be the person. All of these were things…we had no choice in the matter. So we had to do it. It was traditional but it was very structured and it was expected of us.

That's basically how I grew up in it. As far as the church that I've chosen here, it's basically somewhat in that tradition. But not where anything is forced on you. The reason why I think that I chose this church is because this church actually does things in the community that I want to see get done. And they've reached out to the community, which they didn't have to. We're talking about a church of over five thousand members that don't have to come out in Northeast Central Durham and do anything if they didn't want to. But they have reached out to the community. We are probably one of probably about twenty (African Americans). I like it. Basically, I have no problems with it. I enjoy it. The congregation, the people there, I feel like they're very open and honest. I just feel comfortable. I don't have a problem with it. And my kids thoroughly enjoy it. So that's basically how I got involved. When I saw this church going around in the community picking up kids to introduce them to things that were going on in the church I said, "Hmm. That's interesting."

I've gone to all of the churches, visited, trying to find a church that I could associate myself with, Afro-American church. I couldn't find it. It just wasn't there. I'd go to church and I just wouldn't feel like that's where I wanted to be. So it worked for me. It kind of drew me in. You had Mr. Brown that kind of kept tugging at me saying, "Can you help me do this and do that." Then, finally, I just kind of hooked up with him. We raised tobacco. We raised corn, wheat.

Anything that you can name, we raised it. We never really had to purchase anything. The only thing that we had to actually purchase for our household was sugar. Everything else we raised. We raised wheat. We'd take the wheat to market and we had flour. We raised corn. We'd take the corn to market. We did all the marketing. We raised tobacco. We would take our crop in. We'd take our crop in at the end of the year. We'd take it to market, sell it and we made money. So we made money. It wasn't nothing for me to have $1,000 in my pocket to go school shopping. I'm talking about a kid that was about ten or eleven years old. That was easy money.

It was hard work, but the payoff. There was a payoff. You'd work on this crop for about two or three months and then when the payoff—that was the ultimate payoff, what you brought in. That was the good part. We had times that—I think one time we made money and we were going to shop, my brothers, myself and my aunt. We stopped and bought a car. We had that much money on us. We all pooled our funds, bought a car, continued to go shopping, came back, picked the car up on the way back home and went home with a car. Yeah. I think we were. Like I said it was hard work. A lot of people wouldn't have dealt with it because it was hard work. Most people wouldn't want to get up at five o'clock in the morning and go milk a cow before they go to school…stuff like that. They couldn't see that. We had tobacco. So we raised tobacco. If we had to move some tobacco from one place to the other, we would have to get up in the morning before we go to school and move that tobacco, then go home and get ready for school. Well, the way we look at it, my baby brother seemed to get out of most of the work. I think my perspective is the fact that they had him from the time he was six months old. That was almost like saying this is your child. You had him, whereas when we came to them we were already established. That's what I would say. We were ready for school. No diapers, none of that stuff. So we were there, and it just seemed like he never got the blunt end of most of the work. He seemed somehow to get out of it. And we always had to do double the work to take up his slack.

Most of the time it wasn't no different from between you were a boy or a girl you had to do the work if it was given to you. If you were told to do it you did it regardless. The only thing that my aunt believed in—now I had an aunt that believed in strict things. Males do this and girls do this. She had certain things like housework. That was the role of a female. That was not the role of a male. The outside work belongs to the boys; the inside work belongs to the girls. And she had that belief. That may be why my brother can't boil an egg now…because he just—he didn't have to do that stuff. They never had to do that. Even down to picking up their dirty laundry. I mean, none of that. That wasn't their thing. They didn't have to do that. They didn't have to make beds. They didn't have to pick up dirty laundry. They didn't have to do nothing like that because…she had defined roles.

My uncle actually raised his baby sister because when his mother died, his sister was a baby. There was six of us in the household. So it was always somebody in the house. Then my aunt, she worked. She had a job outside of the farm. My uncle had a job outside of the farm. He was a [deputy] sheriff. They worked. They had jobs outside of the farm. Even though we had the farm he worked. He was a deputy sheriff in Yanceyville for years. He recently just retired. It hadn't been but a couple of years since he retired, but he was doing that. She worked for people in Burlington. She had prominent people that she would go and work in their homes all week long. She worked for the lady that owned Sellars Department stores in Burlington, until that lady died. The first family that she worked with—the Moores—they're a very prominent family in Burlington, very prominent, a lot of money. She worked for them for years until his first wife died. She raised their kids and everything. When his first wife died he married again and I don't think her and the second wife got along too well, so that's when she moved over to working for the other lady.

The race relationships in Caswell County…right now until this day they're still kind of stagnant. They're like, you still basically—you have—it's right down the middle, black and white. You still have black people that still sharecrop. And you still have white people that still own the land, and have the working for them. I don't think that's ever going to change. That's going to continue to be because it's such a small town. I lived on a road that didn't have but one white person that lived on it. His wife now—point blank, his wife was a racist. But he wasn't. His wife didn't want to deal with nobody on that road. But he did. He just loved us to death. We actually raised a crop of tobacco together one year. And he was cool. He enjoyed everybody. He helped anybody that he could help. And his wife just couldn't stand it.

Integration

When I started school in Caswell County I came in right at the beginning of integration. Now that was a hard one. I remember a time that there was a parent that got upset because her daughter and I were friends. And that's when we first start integrating schools. She was very upset because she didn't feel like her daughter needed to have any black friends. We went through that and I know how it felt. It affected me in the sense where it made me hostile. But at the same time I understand where my boundaries are. I know my boundaries. People fear what they don't understand. People live a certain way most of their lives and then all of a sudden here's this big change. Okay. Black kids got to go to school with white kids. We're talking about a rural area. Ride the bus with whites and blacks had to ride the bus together.

It had gotten so bad that the white kids, their parents either would buy them cars so they could drive to school and wouldn't have to ride the bus with them or they would take them to school. The only white kids that rode the bus with us were the kids who were unfortunate enough not to have the resources. That was very few, very few that ever rode the bus with us. Yeah, basically that's what it was. And there was very few that would ride with us. We never had to ride with any white kids most of the time because they—the parents just didn't want them. So we went through that whole change. I've seen it from both ends. I remember incidents where parents would get upset with other parents. If we would have activities that go on at school and you had to have both sets of kids involved in it. They would get upset and they would come to school and they would fuss with the principal. Parents would argue with each other. We'd have field days. If some parents saw their kids playing with too many black kids they would say something. Stuff like that. It was going on. Right in our face. It got better. I think it got better after I started middle school. It wasn't too obvious then.

Integration started when I started in first grade. That was a historically black school, the school that I started out in. But at the time that I came in they were just getting ready to open the doors and just open it to everybody. Then they opened the doors and said, "Okay. We can't have this anymore." So went through the integration period.

When I got to my last year of high school, my aunt and uncle decided they wanted to get a divorce. Then my aunt decided, okay, we're going to get a divorce. I'm moving to Burlington. Because that's where she worked for those people. All her connections were in Burlington. So we moved to Burlington for a year. I did my last year of high school at Walter Williams in Burlington. I hated it, too. I think for the first two days of school I rebelled. I said, "I'm not going. I'm dropping out. I'm not going because you took me away from my friends. I don't want to go to school." I sat at home for about two days and I had nobody to entertain me. I went to school. This is not fun at all. You're at home and everybody else is in school. So, it wasn't no fun being at home by yourself. So I got up and I said, "Well I'm going to school." But that just devastated me. I had to leave all of my friends that I had went to school with for years, from day one.

We moved smack in the heart of the city, right in the heart. It was like a big transition and getting used to new people, which was good because, once I got into it, it was all right with me. And once I got into it I met new people and new kids. Then it gave me a broader base of people because coming from Caswell County, where you just were focused on the people that you grew up around, people you'd seen all your life. Then I went to Burlington and then that's when I first met my first person from Taiwan. Then starting meeting different people.

Walter Williams was a predominantly white school. Cummings was the black school. That's the school I actually wanted to go to but I was in the wrong district. So I couldn't go to Cummings so I ended up at Walter Williams. And I rebelled against that. I was like, "I can't go here. That's not the school I need to be at" because all my friends went to Cummings. So then once I got to Walter Williams I enjoyed it. It was okay. I didn't have a problem with it. It turned out to be the best school I ever went to. After I got into it and just said, "Forget it." I was just going to not have these hang ups anymore. It wasn't as bad as I thought. I guess that's what worked for me. Then I was a senior so it couldn't have been but so bad because I was a senior. I had all the privileges. You could leave campus for lunch and all that stuff. So being a senior might have helped. I got through that period and then moved on to something else.

After that then my aunt decided she wanted to move back to—she wanted to move back to Caswell County. So we moved back to Caswell County. After she got divorced she just couldn't take it being in the city, wanted to go back to the country. So she moved right back to Caswell County. The farm still was there. The farm wasn't going anywhere.

When we moved back I was like, "Now what am I going to do? I'm graduated. What do I want to do?" I tried Guilford Tech for a while. I said, "No, that's not going to get it." I was missing something. It was that spirit. I was missing something. So I needed an adventure spirit. I've always been adventurous, so I had to venture out. I decided I was going to leave. When I graduated mostly everything I got was cash. All of my gifts and stuff was cash. I didn't want no gifts, just give me cash. That's what I want. So I took the money and got me a bus ticket. I left. I got a bus ticket and I started out in Baltimore, Maryland. I got a bus ticket to Baltimore, Maryland, stayed in Baltimore for a year, but Baltimore was just not the place for me. It didn't appeal to me. So I left Baltimore and I went to New Jersey, stayed in New Jersey about, almost a year. I have a brother out there. I have a half-brother that lives in New Jersey. So, I'm saying, "Well, this might do." And something about New Jersey didn't get it. About a year later I went to New York. I said, "Well let me go back home to my real home." So when I got to New York I thoroughly enjoyed that for a while. I worked with a veterinarian in Larchmont. So, I lived in New Rochelle, worked in Larchmont. I had this little Jewish veterinarian and he actually wanted me to go to school. He was going to pay for me to go to school. That was my first love, veterinarian medicine. I really said that was what I was going to do when I graduated from high school…that was after my first real actual concrete job that I actually stuck with.

I said that was my real job because it was doing something I loved. I love animals. So it was actually doing something that I loved to do or deal with, so I worked with animals. It was kicking in and nobody but me. I could handle that. So kind of messed around in New York for a little while. I guess.

Coming to Durham

When I turned twenty-seven on my way to twenty-eight, I was like, "I need to do something different now." I said, "I need to go back home" and I really had no plans of ever coming back to North Carolina.

Actually, when I left I was on vacation. I didn't intend to stay here in North Carolina. My brother, my younger brother was graduating from high school and I hadn't been home in like three or four years. I had always called. I would come as far as Virginia and call and say, "I'm on my way," and never make it to North Carolina. I'd turn around and go back—turn around and go back. I called and said I'm coming. I came home, stayed a while, hung out with my friends, my cousins and stuff. That's how I met my husband. I met him in Roxboro. I was minding my own business just jogging down the highway, getting some exercise. And he just came riding by. Just like that, just came riding by and I guess the rest is history. We've been together ever since. I called my job and the strangest thing—I called my job and told them I missed my bus but I'd be on the next one. Never caught that bus. I was on vacation, wasn't planning on staying in North Carolina. I had no plans on it.

I said, "Well I'll come stay a while and go back." And ended up spending the rest of my time here. I guess that's love. I just kind of made my way on to Durham and Dexter Hughes. Born and bred in Roxboro. And then how you tell yourself it's time for you to do something else with your lifetime, for you to settle down. But I didn't want to settle down with anybody from the city. I said, "Nah. I'm going to get me a country man." I just said, well I need a man from the country. I don't need a man from the city. I don't want to even go that route. I'd probably be divorced three or four times. So I went through that and just kind of trickled on my way to Durham, ended up in Durham. There wasn't any job opportunities (in Roxboro).

When I was in Roxboro I was driving over here to work because I started out working at Darryl's out of Roxboro before it was the Greenery and all that stuff. I was actually driving over here every day. I was over here most of the night because I had friends over here at Durham. I needed to move to Durham. There's no need of me staying in Roxboro and trying to be over here. So that's how I ended up in Durham. I have one cousin that lives here. I didn't have any family here other than my cousin.

Well I moved here first because he was in service. He was in the army. When he got out he came to Durham. That's how I ended up here—kind of worked odd different jobs like Darryl's. I worked at the Greenery over by Duke. First I was hotel hopping. I was like doing the hotels. I was doing the Brownstone, the Sheraton. I was bail person. I told them, "Don't ever call me a bail man." I was a bail person. I met a lot of people through that. I met a lot because a lot of people come in here on that rice diet. Had a lot of friends, a lot of friends, when I was at the Brownstone. I met so many people. I met this one guy (he's dead now). His name was Mr. Clement. He had a lot of money. He was from Texas. He actually came to Durham to be on that rice diet so he could have this hernia operation. He met this girl that had an advertising agency. This man was almost eighty years old, never been married. All he ever did was made money, never been married. He met this girl named Jane that had an advertising agency. She was like thirty-eight and he married her.

So Jane sold the advertising agency and invited me to the wedding. I went to the wedding and everything. I've met a lot of interesting people through the hotel. I like meeting people. That's one of my pet peeves [*sic*] just to meet different people all the time. And I never meet a stranger. I try not to. Never meet a stranger. Treat you like I've known you all my life. I've just kind of met with a lot of people at the hotel. I had people that'd come in and they'd kind of come in and be on a diet for about six months and they'd leave. Always looking for me when they come back to town. I mean, a lot of people, a lot that way.

I think I ended up at the Greenery. It started out as a nursing home but then it turned into a rehabilitation center. I went from the Greenery to Carolina Re-Entry—a head injury program on Morehead. I don't know what my position was called. I kind of did a little bit of everything. It was like I came in under transportation, kind of taking clients back and forth to doctors' appointments and rehab and then, it just kind of escalated to a whole bunch of other stuff.

I met a lot of interesting people that way. A lot of people coming in that had different head injuries from different parts of the state, country and whatever. I met people that way, met their families, kind of got used to them. People still call me, they still call me and write me now. It's networking. That's what I'm about. I've got clients now—I've got clients now that if they see me, I still have to keep in touch with them to see how they're doing. I actually have one client that I worked for about a year after I left the Greenery—after I left the Carolina I worked for him about a year. He stays in Gary. He had an aneurysm. Before he had his aneurysm, he was the CEO of one of the major corporations, finance companies in the state. He told me one day, "If I'd known then what I know now I would have stopped working so hard and I'd have slowed down and took life a little bit easier." I worked for him for about a year. And I still stay in contact with him. He lives in Gary. I keep up with him, see how he's doing.

He was partial paralyzed. He had paralysis on one side so I kind of helped him out and gave his wife a break. When I'd come in I'd tell her to just leave. I've got him. You go do what you what to do. We'd go out, and eat and take him out. Take him out riding and do stuff with him. And I had a client up in Chapel Hill, another client. He was actually the head pathologist over at UNC? He was the pathologist. He was the head person over at the morgue. Well not the morgue, but at UNC autopsies—where they do the autopsies. Yeah. And he had an aneurysm, too. His wife just gave him to me. See, once they'd leave there I did such a good job, they'd be like, "Well come work for me."

I had my son in 1986. About that time, you have to take a second look at life. Once you have children it's totally different. What are we going to do now? When you don't have children you can just do that kind of stuff. You can network or do anything else you want to do. Once my son was old enough to be in school especially when my oldest one did his first year in school, that's when I realized. I was still working at the head injury program. I was like, "Well I need to be accessible to my kids." That's the one thing I said, I'm going to be accessible. I don't need a job bogging me down where I have to if I need to be somewhere for my child I have to get permission from the job.

A lot of jobs don't like you taking off all the time. I said, "Now what can I do?" So that's when I started volunteering in the school. I quit my job and started doing catering at home. I was still doing the home health care stuff because I had a great in-home daycare lady. That's one thing that I wouldn't say that I had the best childcare. I never had to put my kids in daycare. I had this person that if I had to be at work at four o'clock in the morning she'd spend the night at my house. I mean I didn't have a problem. I never had a problem with childcare. That was one thing I was blessed with. I had somebody that was reliable. It was all in-home.

So I didn't have to take them out of their environment and I had my other son. They're only like twenty-three months apart. So they're close in age—almost two years apart. When I was taking him to school, the other one, I was taking him to school with me. He'd go right along with me. That's how he got an early start on things. So...fortunate enough to have a good kindergarten teacher and got him in school for a day. I felt worse than he did leaving. So then I thought, "What can I do? I've got to come up with something that I can do that allows me to be accessible." So I started catering from home. Starting doing lunches for the teacher. I started out taking lunches to school to the teachers because I looked at the market. I said teachers can't leave and go get lunch. But a lot of times they get tired of cafeteria food.

So there's a market for it. All you have to do is be a person that delivered. All I had to do is get a menu together and offer it to them each week. So my girlfriend and I had a first rough draft menu I put together and took it up to the school. And I said, "I've got some lunches if anybody's interested." The first lunches for the first week I took free just to expose them to people and let

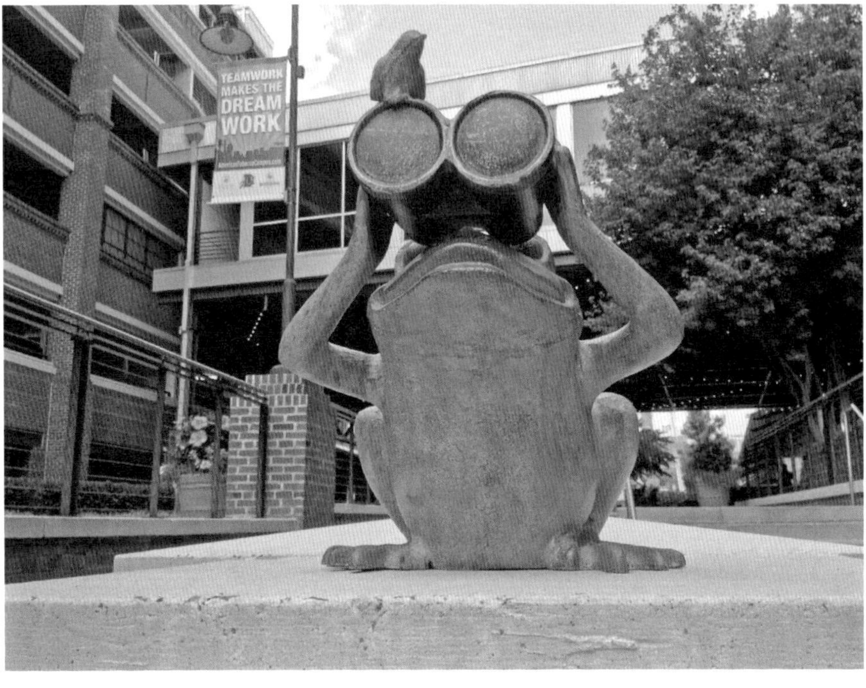

Durham today: The American Tobacco Campus in Durham is now a tourism magnet. *Photograph by the author.*

people know what they'd be missing. So once I started doing that then, I got this call from people that wanted the lunches and I started bringing lunches. And I was selling, doing pretty good.Then other people started calling up. I had clients at the Lincoln Center, clients at Blue Cross/Blue Shield, clients at Becton Dickinson. I had clients, basically, all over Durham. I was taking lunches. My catch was that I would deliver. I would bring it to you. All you had to do was call it in before 12 o'clock and I'd have it ready. I had a menu, a weekly menu.

And it went on for a while and then my girlfriend moved to Michigan, so that left me on my own. I tried to do it for a while, but it was hard preparing and delivering. I couldn't find another reliable person. You have to have a reliable partner when you're doing stuff like that. I still have people now want to know when I'm going to get started again. They still want those lunches. I was good at it. Everything that I do involves some networking. Meanwhile I've still got all these people that I've networked with by bringing them lunches. Went from lunches to just being at school everyday volunteering.

I started at Fayetteville Street volunteering, was in there volunteering every day. If I didn't walk through the doors, the kids didn't. Then I moved on this side of town. I moved from that side of town where Fayetteville Street in that district to this side of town. So then that's when I started Holloway Street School. That's how I started networking at East End and kind of networking the community because when you do afterschool programs you've got to know the community. People come and get their kids. And if you do a good job, people want you. I started doing summer camps. I worked with summer camps. The older my kids got it got more involved, more intense. See, what I do basically…I base it on how it reflects on my kids. That's how I do what I do.

I make decisions based on my kids. I want my children to grow up in an environment like some of these areas. From working in the environment of East End and Holloway, I've learned that education is a strong point for a lot of the families. For a lot of the kids it's not something they feel like they need. I'm talking about generations of people that just feel like education is the last thing they want to be bothered with. They're dropouts. Their mothers were dropouts. Their grandparents were dropouts and it's continuing down. I ask kids, "What are you going to be?" I actually question kids about what they plan on being when they grow up and they don't have a clue. The first time a little girl told me that she was going to work at the Red Roof Inn. Her mother was going to get her a job at the Red Roof Inn. Now something needs to be done to change the way of thinking. I'm not saying it's not a reputable job, but at the same time, set your sights higher. Your goals have to be high. You can't say, "Well, if I work at the Red Roof Inn, that's major work for me." If you ask any of those kids, that go to these neighboring schools, their goals are not high. You need people out there that encourage them—even if their family don't—to have goals. I tell my kids in my house I don't accept Bs. Even though most people say, "Well you don't accept a B?" I said, "No. If I accept a B then they're going to come in with a C." If I accept a C the next thing's going to be a D. If I set the sights high then that means that you'll be on the A honor roll most of the time if I set them high. So I set most of the goals high.

Education—now one thing mom and them told me, they said, "If you don't do nothing else in life, graduate from high school." See when I grew up, graduating from high school was a major step. If you graduate from high school you've accomplished [something]. College wasn't a real biggie, but high school was, high school was a must. You had to do that. They believed that when you go to school, you do your best. I'm not going to have that foolishness. They didn't want no reports coming home. I know one time I got a report card and I had a bad grade on there. I think I had a bad grade. I almost died. I tried to change the grade. I couldn't take that home. I was like, "Oh, lord, they're going to kill me when I get home." I couldn't take them home. I was trying to figure out how to change it. I'm like the rest of the kids. It was important. You didn't get in trouble at school. I feel like if you lower your standards, then you're not going to accomplish anything. You're not going to accomplish your goals, the

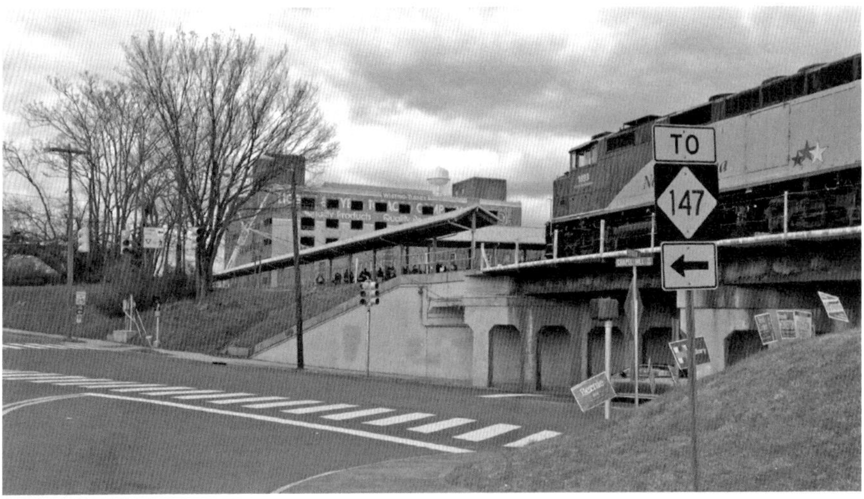

Durham today: The Durham train station stands before the Liggett & Myers building, under renovation. Tobacco's role in the Durham economy has virtually disappeared, as the community long ago rebranded itself the "City of Medicine," referencing the world-class Duke Medical Center and its sprawling campus of specialty hospitals. *Photograph by the author.*

goals that you set up. I'm not going to lower my standards regardless. They'll get upset but they'll appreciate it when they get eighteen when they have that full academic scholarship at Duke, full athletic scholarship at UNC. They'll appreciate it. So we have goals. So I just kind of push them.

I was working doing afterschool programs and summer camps and then I started subbing. Because I was in the school and I knew the kids. The teachers kept saying, "Well will you watch my class?" I said, "Well if I'm going to watch your class I might as well get paid for it." So then I started subbing. Then there became a high demand for me because they know, give me your roughest classes. I pride myself on going into your roughest classes. I don't like easy classes. I like the ones where they say the kids are out of control. Those are the classes I like to deal with. So I like going. I ended up going and it was high demand because you can't find subs anymore. People don't want to go into it. They'll tell you, "I'm not going to that school. I'm not going to that class." You've got a lot of classes that don't have teachers a lot of times. That's how I got kind of wrapped up in that whole educational thing. My driving force that got me involved in community stuff was Carl Washington. He's deceased now. He was actually second in charge of Durham Parks and Recreation. He was a strong advocate for Northeast Central Durham. He actually was one of the founders of Northeast Central Durham. It was founded in 1994.

He just knew what the need was in the community. Northeast Central Durham and this whole area has been deemed the most socially deprived. They done studies and they decided that most of the crime is coming from this area. Everything is in this area. So, a lot of people get a lot of grants and make a lot of money off of Northeast Central Durham. They started out having these PAC (Partners Against Crime) meetings. The first PAC meeting started at the Antioch Church down here on Holloway Street. I think I attended one or two of them. Pretty interesting. Sounds okay. Most of my community work was being done at Edgemont, not doing it with Northeast Central Durham. Kind of pulling some things together working with people and then all of a sudden Carl came.

He called me up one day. I don't know where he come up with calling, but he called me up and invited me to lunch. I was just wondering what he wanted with me. He asked me would I be interested in being a part of Northeast Central Durham. It was about the second year Northeast Central Durham was established (around 1996). They were ready to elect new chair people, new officers and he came to me and he asked me. He said, "We need new blood in this organization and I feel like you can add something to it." He asked me would I be interested in being a chair. I was like, I don't know about all of that. I have to wonder about it. I'll have to think about it. And I finally, I said, "Well, throw my name in the hat," never thinking that I'd get voted in. I actually established this group called Padlock, was one of the founders of it. We were actually doing a Saturday tutorial where we just came together as parents. We had nobody else involved in it. We didn't have any outside people. We funded it. We went out and got people—we went out and got our volunteers and everything. We were actually doing a tutorial every Saturday where a few of us parents from Edgemont would meet. We would tutor kids. But it was nontraditional tutoring. We did tutoring—everything from math, reading and everything into it.

It was working and people were hearing about it. I mean it was booming. The Saturday tutorial we were doing for the kids in the neighborhood. No requirements to be in there, just be a neighborhood kid. We didn't have as much support parent wise. We just kind of got at a standstill where at any point where we could start back up. All decisions were made by parents. It took on a life of its own. We put together a group working with women over there in public housing and anybody else that wanted to be involved. Where you meet once a week and we discuss social—any issues that they have, we put them on the table. We discuss them and try to figure out how to deal with them. They'd have everything from housing, boyfriends, children, anything. It was an open group. We kind of dealt with different issues. That group still is going on. They still meet once a week. I think they're doing stuff like ceramics. It was a good concept. We incorporated that concept, too. We actually went and incorporated. Now I've got a new—got a new group called BAHAA. That's Blacks and Hispanics Are Alike. That's the latest one. That's incorporated. It started a year ago when the Latino population at East Way (Elementary) started growing. I think that's where it got to me at its most—at its highest rate, I think, at East Way.

I was basically sitting on the front door step every morning at East Way when the doors opened at 7:30. Standing outside, opening the door, letting kids out of cars, whatever it took, greeting parents trying to get them involved in school and things that go on in school. We established Parents on Patrol at East Way. That's where I had a group. I had a sturdy group of parent volunteers that came in every morning and every afternoon and manned the hallways, the entrance and exit and did things, kind of helped teachers out in classrooms—the whole nine yards. Parents on Patrol. Incorporated that one, too. I haven't got an idea that I don't incorporate because I know people take your ideas and make money. So I have to incorporate so nobody can take that concept.

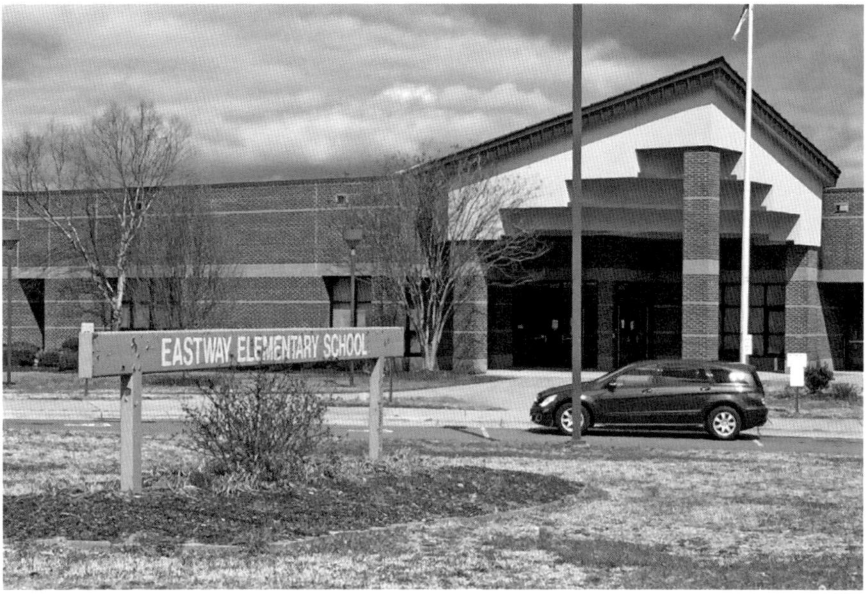

Durham today: East Way Elementary School in Northeast Central neighborhood. *Photograph by the author.*

Anybody can use the concept but they have to get the permission. And that's why I have to incorporate everything. We did Parents on Patrol, that's still going on. But the BAHAA is the latest. I'm trying to take that school wide, the concept. See the idea of us establishing a group was to improve relations between black parents and Latino parents at East Way because there were none. There were no relations. It was like two different environments. There was never any connection. It was like we got to figure out a way to connect these because the one thing we got in common is these kids we bring through the door every day. So we had a breakfast one morning and we talked about the group. When the group started it didn't have a name. It was just basically a group that was meeting.

We started out meeting once a week. Basically, we sit down…we would teach them basic English and we'd teach them basic Spanish. We just wanted basic conversation of English and Spanish. We didn't need all of that other stuff at Durham Tech. We just need conversation so that when we see each other we can at least greet each other and ask you how you're feeling and whatnot. I think after we'd done that for a couple of weeks we started potluck Fridays. Basically on Wednesday, whenever we learned on Wednesday we'd have breakfast on Friday. And we'd use what we learned on Wednesday on

Friday. We actually started doing on Friday with our breakfast is inviting people in, different people to come to our breakfast on Friday to bring information to the parent, Latino and black. We had landlords coming because they had issues about housing.

We were inviting people that we knew we had issues with. So we were inviting landlords. We had a couple of times we had city council, Lorisa [Seibel] came. Whatever issues that they had if we had a meeting on Wednesday and say somebody has something that they were talking about that was an issue, then I said, "Well let me see who I can get to come." We even had the Mary Kay lady come and do facials. Whatever we had issues about we'd bring people in. So we started inviting different people in on our breakfasts. Then the word got out about the group. And Channel 5 came in and decided to do a story on us. Now once Channel 5 did a story on us, we had senior citizens coming over to East Way wanting to get in on the group. Then they did an article in the *Herald-Sun*. And that gave us a little more exposure. We went from there and then got more people involved. That's when we started dealing with Will Atwater from Seeds. He heard about it. He wanted to improve his Spanish plus connect, too. So he came in and offered. We started doing the community garden thing, working that into our program.

If you look at the school—the school is a breeding ground for whatever issues that come up because you got parents and children that come through the doors every day. And when those kids and those children come through that door, they have issues. I mean, you have parents that come through the door that may have had a bad night at home. You've got kids that come through the door that may have had to dodge bullets all night. They have issues. When they come through that door, that's the only place they have to deal with those issues. How they deal with them determines how people listen to them. A lot of times when children come into school they act out a certain way. They're acting because they went through something. If their behavior has changed overnight you have to look at, "wonder what happened in this child's life in that—in twenty-four hours" or ever how many hours it took for them to leave school and come back.

Since the first group started, our first core group started, we've had four babies born. We had one baby that died. Right now we got three mothers that, two mothers that's pregnant, having some problems. But see that's what we have to deal with. Out of the group we're dealing with all of the issues, everything that goes on with them. And that was one of the reasons for forming this group because Ms. Perez had brought it to my attention that the kids, the Hispanic kids were afraid when they came to school because when they were at home they wasn't—there was a rash of home invasions on Latinos—because they know they keep large amounts of cash in their homes. The faces that they were seeing that was creating this crime—were provoking crime on them—were black. They'd [be] coming to school and all they're seeing is black faces. They had a fear. They were actually fearing the kids at school because when they went home that's all they saw. They didn't see anything positive going on with black people. They just saw negative kicking the doors in and coming in the house robbing them. Had a couple of kids guns were held to their heads threatening—holding the kids to get money from the parents. Stuff like that. These kids when they came to school, they didn't have no—they didn't have a counselor. We had a counselor, but they weren't going to the counselor saying, "I need to talk" or anything. They were having to deal with that in their own way sitting in school looking at all these black faces around them. That had to be terrifying. So Ms. Perez was telling me about how the kids were feeling. I said, "Well we need to do something about that. If we can convince the parents that it's not all black people then maybe they can convince the children." Doing that has improved relationships because at one time it was tense. Kids don't understand. They're not able to put things in the right perspective. We just put this group together and the group helped. We've got a bunch of friends around.

Every time I need a vote or something I just tell them to come, come, come and vote. And when I say hold your hand up, hold your hand up. It depends on how people feel. We're going to start having it at Holloway Street now that Ms. Perez is now working with housing that gives us a broader range. So we want to open it up to the total community. It was open at East Way. You're talking about a school so that mainly we were dealing with the parents of that school. We want it to be open to anybody in Northeast Central Durham. Like I said we had a good group, really did, formed some good relationships there, went to a couple of parties with them. We started going to birthday parties. They were inviting us to birthday parties and stuff on the weekend at their houses. I invited them to my home. "Come over to my house." We introduced them. Like I said, we learned—they learned how to eat grits, and bacon and eggs and stuff. Whereas I learned how to eat—drink chocalaiti and eat bean burritos for breakfast and whatever else. So, we taught each other something. And that's what it was about. It was understanding cultures.

A lot of things I took for granted at one time. I learned that what is obvious to some people is not so obvious to others. And I learned that from them. A lot of things that I just assumed…I figure you're human just like me, I assume this is not. There's a lot of cultural difference in how they do things, what they

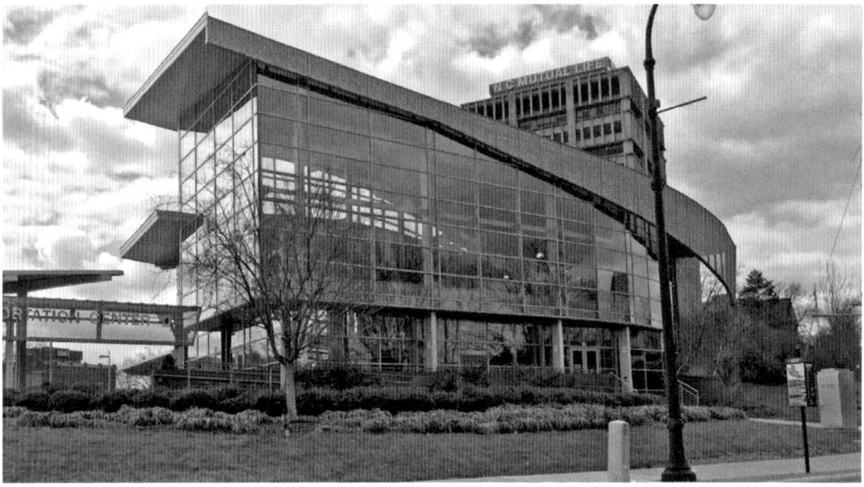

Durham today: Across from the train station sits Durham's bus station and transportation hub, in the shadow of NC Mutual Life Insurance Company. The hub was designed by award-winning architect and Durham resident Phil Freelon. The station replaced the "Heart of Durham" hotel, long in disrepair. *Photograph by the author.*

believe in, the whole nine yards. Well I think the conflict point in the community is just basically how they do things. How things are done in their culture versus how we do—how we're traditionally brought up to do things. When it comes to housing how we live. I wouldn't sit outside and have a twelve-pack on my doorstep and then when I get up I leave the empty cans of twelve-pack out there. That's something I wouldn't do because I wasn't raised that way. And that's not in my culture. But if they do it, who am I to say it's wrong? That's their culture. That's what they have been raised and taught to do. It doesn't make it right and it doesn't make it wrong—just saying that's your culture. Now in understanding what we can do about it. Okay. Let's sit down and talk about how we can better do this, how we can handle this.

That's part of the problem about the housing thing as far as decent housing. We had one landlord that ran us off some property one day. We went advocating for some Latinos. They invited us in. We brought the inspector and the landlord ran us off the property. Told us—called the police, told us to leave because we were bringing attention to him and what he wasn't doing. He said, "I don't know why y'all here complaining. They're living better here than they would be in Mexico." That's the way people generally think. That is actually what people are thinking. They come here from wherever they come from and they're actually living 100 percent better than what they would have been living if they had stayed in their country. If they're living in a house that has substandard heat, substandard plumbing or whatever. That's okay because that's a step up from what they were. It's justifying what you're doing and what you're not doing. That's what we heard a lot of. Then at the same time, Hispanics are going to have to understand that, we understand that this is your culture and how you do things, but at the same time, you're moving into a culture and a way of living and other people expect certain things.

It's going to have to be give and take on both sides. A lot of times folks are not willing to give and take. Whether or not Hispanics are taking jobs that historically African Americans have held. It's an issue. It's an issue because what has happened is the job market now that used to be dominated by Afro-American is not anymore because when we start asking for more money because of the economics, then they're saying, "Well I can have me two or three Mexicans. I don't need to pay you this amount. I can take what I pay you and split it in half and get two people to do this." Now that's the theory. That's the theory of the employers, too. The employers know this. So it's not so much that we as Afro-Americans believe that they're taking our jobs. Employers are actually allowing that to happen. They're feeding into that concept, too. They'd rather hire a Hispanic person at a $1.50 less than you would hire me to do the same job because you don't have to pay any taxes on this person or anything. You've got people working every day that have to take no taxes out of. You're not responsible or anything on it. You just give them a straight up salary. And that's got to be less paperwork on you as an employer, less headache, less money you have to spend. So you benefit more by hiring them. Rather than—say you hire me and I come in and I'm going to the human relation commission and I'm calling the NAACP. Rather than to put up with that headache, I don't have to deal with that. I've got a few Hispanics over here that'll work for next to nothing. So—I guess the shared goals that we have when we're working with the campaign to me, the shared goals that we have that everybody live in decent housing. It's just that simple. Nobody should be subjected to some of the things that we've seen out here when it comes to housing just because you were unfortunate enough not to be a legal citizen or you just happen not to be a person of whatever social standards. Our goal is to make sure that everybody has decent houses and the minimum policies applied should be enforced to help people reach their goal. That's basically what this housing is because this housing, this campaign, we deal with much more than housing. Some of the housing issues that we've dealt with have gotten into things that we never even thought we would imagine we'd have to deal with. We've become social workers. We're dealing with people of issues that go far and beyond a leaky toilet stool or something like that. We're just dealing with a lot of issues. That's why I say this campaign as far as like the campaign itself speaks for itself. It is a campaign. It goes beyond housing.

We started East Way—they started a housing project to build houses in the area of Few Gardens. It was the East Way Home Ownership. That came through Northeast Central Durham. What happened was we couldn't sell the houses because of the neighborhood. People are not going to purchase a $60,000 home and you got four or five boarded houses right beside it and crime and everything else. So, it was like, we can't sell these houses. What are we going to do? We've got a development started here, can't do anything with it right now. The only thing that we're selling at this point is the Habitat houses. Habitat for Humanity. You can basically give those away. So, you can get a house in Habitat. This is two years now. So that was around the same time as BAHAA started. Well when Lorisa came to me, basically, I got involved in this from the beginning. She called us up and we talked about it. We talked about the issues, because basically everything we're doing here we have been doing all along in the community. We needed a stronger group that could go before the housing appeal board and go before the housing department. We needed a stronger group. So we just felt like if we pooled our resources and all our support then we could make more of an impact. Rather than just, got two or three individuals over here in Northeast Central Durham that's going down there talking to whoever and not really getting anything accomplished.

It was just a collaboration of the different people who were doing the same thing in their community. It's diverse, a very diverse group. We even got some slumlords. We've got one—I have to give him credit because I wouldn't have showed up if I was him, but he has been coming. And he's been coming to the meetings and he has been participating. He's taken an interest in it because he knows there are problems. We have to hear from both sides. We can't just dump it all on the landlords and say, "Well, you should be doing this and doing that" and just get radical. So we understand that landlords have issues, too. You've got a piece of property. You can't make money off it if you have to continue to put repairs into it from other people's neglect. We understand that.

This campaign is basically to create a bond where you don't have just radical groups attacking different people. You've got a radical group attacking a landlord. You've got a radical group attacking the Hispanics. You've got radical groups—we want one group that can deal with all the issues and deal with it in a manner where it's civil and not real out there. So that's what the campaign does; the campaign kind of deals with the issues on a level head. More than a dozen people involved. These are all your sponsors. We started out with probably about just a small list right there and just people have bought into the concept. Over the last two years all these people have— they bought in. They got on board. It's making our group strong. It's making it strong to the point that we're right now in the process of trying to get some policies changed at state level when it pertains to houses.

We're trying to get some things in place here in Durham. That's why we needed a stronger group with more diversity in it. To have some impact you have to do that. One or two people they say, "Here come the radical people again, that trouble maker." I've heard that all the time, so you have to have a lot of support. That's why I like the network. What is it about you or your family make up or what you've experienced that you care enough to do this? When I deal with people I think people have gotten the understanding that I'm not a person that's going to come and try to judge your situation. I'm only here to help you deal with whatever you're dealing with in the best manner it can be dealt with. I'm not going to try to steer you wrong. I'm going to try to help you. If I can't help you I'm going to try to lead you to the people that you need to be talking to. Why does it matter to you to make a difference?

I guess what I'm getting at is...a lot of people who are pretty comfortable, pretty secure, don't have to do this. I mean you could not do this. You could just attend to your children. I do have to do it because, like I tell people, it only takes one paycheck to put you in the same situation of people. I mean people just don't see it that way. It could take one flick of the switch and you could be right there in that spot of those people that are having all these difficulties. It doesn't take much. A lot of people think that once they reach that peak of society that they want to be at, "Oh nothing can tear me down and I don't have to look at those people. So why should I be bothered?" At the same time I look at it like this. I live here. I don't plan on going anywhere. And every time I step out my door I see people living a certain way. It's beneath me because of the way I was raised. I just can't believe that people, other people, would allow people to live a certain way. It just seems like everybody should have some kind of compassion. You look at your family. You may have reached that peak but it doesn't mean everybody in your family has. Finding that one person in your family that hasn't reached it. I mean just put yourself in those people's position. And that's what I do. I try to put myself in their position and see how I would feel. I know how I feel. That's why I go deal with people. I go out in the community. I talk to people. I let people know I'm here if you need me. I'm open. I'm not trying to hide

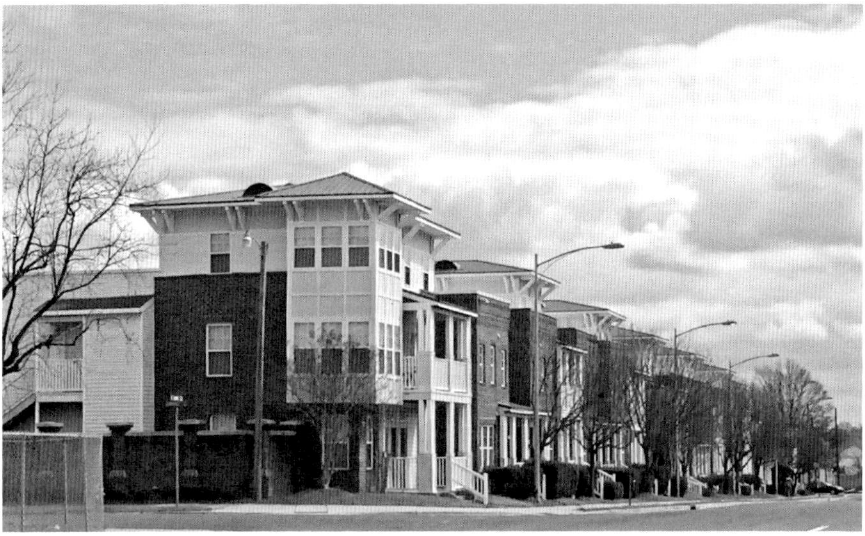

Durham today: The HOPE VI housing development, built by the Durham Housing Authority in 2000, helped the city to spur new housing and commercial development downtown and into the Northeast Central neighborhood. *Photograph by the author.*

nothing from you. I'm not trying to use you. I'm not trying to make money off you or nothing like that. I'm just here.

That's one of the things maybe the media needs to put a muzzle on and stop doing that. They don't talk about the good stuff that go on. It just tears the community apart. I mean if you keep us not getting along you'll always make money. There'll always be some financial gain from it. You can always have people that come in and have these well-intended ideas. And say, oh well, let me go over there and do this little survey on Northeast Central Durham when it relates to blacks and Hispanics and I'll write this little proposal. Everybody has their own interest and their own ulterior motives. That's why I'm with an organization that basically every time somebody wants to come in and do a study or get some money, they have to come to us. They have to come to Northeast Central Durham and ask us to support them.

If you want to write a grant and you want to get that grant approved and get that money, if you came to Northeast Central Durham and we support it, you're guaranteed to get that money. People may have good intentions and might want to do something. It makes us very skeptical of people coming in. People think we're being hard. It's because we feel like we're being used as guinea pigs. People come in and say okay, we just these need these demographics. We need these people. We are being used as lab rats. That's what has happened to this community. It's like this community has been used so much. In the process of being used we don't benefit nothing out of it. I mean we don't even get the help that supposedly the people come in and say help they going to give us. They end up getting what they want financially and they end up leaving us. And most of the time they leave us in worse shape than when they came in. They use us to that point.

SOLUTIONS

Get more community people involved in the process. We can do that. If there's going to be some financial gain. One of Northeast Central Durham's goals—we have missions and goals. One of our goals is to decrease unemployment. Our mission is to provide quality education, decrease substandard housing, the whole nine yards, economic development. We have missions and goals. In order to meet those goals, if you got people coming in getting million dollar grants off of us, using us and getting it and we don't get anything out of it—not even a job, not even a prospects of a job—then what did we—what purpose did we serve other than a lab rat. We served no purpose. I mean if it's just that simple. At some point you got to look at, okay, if you come in here and say you want to make some money off us, what do we get out of it. When you leave is the community going to have a park sitting over here that's safe for our kids to go into and play? Is the community going to have a center over here we can do tutoring and all that? What are we going to get out of it? That's what we want to see. And that's basically where we're at now. When anybody comes in we tell them, well what do we plan on, what do we receive from this? Are there any benefits that we can say that's tangible? That's something that you can tell us, well, just to study. We want tangible stuff. We want to know what we benefit from this. Most of Northeast Central Durham has really gotten fed up with people coming in with good intentions. They really have. The taste is really bad and they don't like it.

We had a person come for instance want to do an alcohol and wine study. We know who sells the most malt liquor. We know where all the malt liquor and wine is sold in Northeast Central Durham. We know where the majority of convenience stores that sell in Northeast Central Durham. Now, what else are you going to come in and add to this? Nothing. It's already been done. So who are you benefiting? And that's where we're at. My goal is to help other people: other get employment, other people get out of poverty. I mean you can't make it out of poverty at $5.50 an hour. You can't do it. It's impossible. I mean, it's work to work first. This work from welfare to independent, it's not going to work. All you're going to do is promote a bigger problem especially in communities like this because you got most of your welfare recipients in communities like this. So you're going to have a problem. When they cut out AFDC and this Work First there's going to be a big rash of crime that's going to drop and then that paper's going to be full of stuff. It's going to happen. I mean, you're taking people off the system that's been on the system for years, no skills, no nothing, and you're saying just because they have to go to work, they got to go to work. And they're going to go to work making $5.50 an hour with four, five or more kids in the household can't support. You can't do it. It is impossible. And then they say, well the system says you have to do it. The system is not living over here in Northeast Central Durham. The system is living up on the mountain. Most people that are sitting there dictating would not even set foot in these areas. So the system doesn't work. And that's why you have to have people out there that care, that's going to work for the community. In the process of these people coming in wanting to do things and all these well intentions, they're going to have to involve the community. They have to let the community have some involvement.

You still have people getting robbed. That's going to continue as long as we have people and no jobs. But that decrease alone from not seeing it always in the paper made me believe that there has been some improvement. Basically people want fair and decent housing. They want jobs that provide decent income. They want safe neighborhoods for their kids to grow up. They want decent education. I mean, basically the goals are the same of all of us. I don't think there's much of a difference. I don't think there's any difference. That's my perspective. I just think the way we perceive it is the only difference. As far as how it's done, I mean, if we start looking at things as more collaborative efforts and start doing things as a unit, together, we can accomplish more. Because like they say, united we stand, divided we fall. And that's what happens every time. We get more united regardless of what your ethnic background is. Then we can accomplish a lot more. Then that's—this campaign right here shows that. With all of the support that we have we get more done with this effort. And have these many people involved than if it was just me and Lorisa and maybe one or two other people.

They're not just saying, oh, here comes that group again or here comes that Jackie. Every time I look up here she comes. Here she comes again. And now they're seeing that other people are dealing with these same issues and having these problems. They're dealing with us on a different level. They're looking at us more of an alliance of strength. They're not looking at us as individuals that's just out there being radical trying to stir up stuff. We're stirring the pot and we need to leave alone. That's not happening anymore. They're looking at it as, like I said, NECD is a force to be reckoned with. There's no doubt about that. That's what I say—networking. Go networking. We're networking now. I can't say it's me but I know that working with Northeast Central Durham has improved my understanding of how the system works. A lot of things before I didn't know about and I didn't understand. But now I got the system to an art.

I know how to access the system. So that's just one of the things that you learn. It's a learning experience. What we try to do is we update our board every year. We don't try to keep the same people in position. That's one of our goals. We nominate new people every year. We promote leadership. You can't have the same people always in the same position because then they'll say well, dang they ain't doing anything. They got the same people running that thing. So every year we elect a whole new board of people so that everybody has the opportunity to become leaders in the community. And that's what it's about—promoting leadership. The NECD does that. We can't have the same people. We refuse to.

7

DIANE WRIGHT

Mother didn't want us to learn to hate so she didn't take me to the movies very often for me to have to go up into the balcony and climb all those stairs.

I was born in Louisville, Kentucky, in 1948 and lived there for twenty-two years. Then I moved to Dover, Delaware; Charleston, South Carolina; then Greensboro, North Carolina, for a year before coming to Durham. I had an older sister—eleven years older—now deceased.

My mother was a nurse and my father worked for the post office. He was a parcel postman [letter carrier]. He worked for the post office his whole career.

They tell me I could "pass" [for white] but it's not something I ever tried to do.

Growing Up

When I began school, it began in a black school. I went to kindergarten through second grade there. The Brown case was decided when I was in the second grade. The local superintendent of schools said that they would follow the law and our schools would be desegregated. He said that the first year would be voluntary and then the second year everyone would have to go. So my parents sent me to the white school for third grade and then I skipped fourth grade.

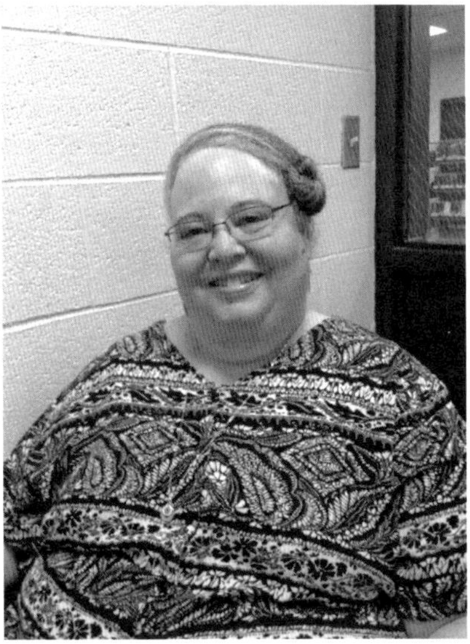

Diane Wright. *Photograph by the author.*

Being with older kids was difficult in junior high school but everything is difficult in junior high school. My mother died just before she was 50 when I was 15 years old; my father died just a couple of years ago, he would be 103 [born 1911]. His father lived to be 104.

The first year when it was voluntary, I guess I could pass because nobody bothered me. I didn't think anything of it. By then, my sister was in college. She went to college when she was fifteen. She went to Fisk on a Ford Foundation scholarship.

Pat's the genius…just ask my mother. She was brilliant and pretty, and she could play any instrument. She could play softball. My mother used to say [of me], "The only thing you have going for you is that you can get along with people."

The second year all the other kids came over in their work, kids in my fourth grade classroom—black kids—and there was teasing and that sort of thing. I would have kids tell me, "Oh you stink," that kind of thing.

And one day I went home and said to my mother, "Mother, what's a nigger?" Because that's the first time I'd ever heard that word. She said, "That's just a word that stupid people use to describe us. Don't you worry about that. You just worry about getting good grades." I said, "OK."

NORTH CAROLINA

Not long after coming to North Carolina, Wright found herself in proximity to an event that stunned the country—the Greensboro Massacre. On November 3, 1979, five protesters were shot and killed by members of the Ku Klux Klan and the American Nazi Party in Greensboro. The demonstrators where participating in a "Death to the Klan" rally against the Klan's violence and were gunned down in broad daylight, with much of it caught on film. Despite that unusual amount and type of evidence (many eyewitnesses and a film showing the killings), the criminal and civil rights trials resulted in acquittals for the defendants. Only civil action that followed brought modest accountability.

I worked with one of the guys at the Department of Social Services (DSS)... that happened the second year that I was here. When I worked in Greensboro I worked at a convenience store so I wasn't mixing with the public the way you do when you work for DSS and you get a feel for the whole community. I was shocked by that. How could that happen? They just gunned these people down? These were nice decent people.

Durham

I had been married and my marriage ended so I came to Durham and found a job. I worked for a convenience store, and they gave me training. On my first night on the job, I was held up at gunpoint. So I kept working because I figured well that's already happened so what else could go wrong?

In a new relationship, I transferred to Greensboro. I did well at work. I got promoted. I got my own store. He worked for 7-Eleven also and he got his own store and they were both in Durham. I worked from February to July 4, and that weekend (the store was not open twenty-four hours) when I came back to work, someone had broken in and stolen the safe. Those things are heavy! If I come early in there in the middle of doing that they would've had no compunction about killing me. So I left for a job in my field. I had been a social worker for five years before I got married. And by December, I found a job at DSS. I worked there for five years, and then I went back to school.

The guy and I had broken up. I had bought a house, and I called him up and said, "I've got a house. Want to come over and let's give it a try?" We got married. That's probably the biggest mistake I made [in] my life. I worked in various jobs in the private sector. I got busy and community organizing when I worked at Edgemont Community Center and then got elected to city council. I served eight years.

The most difficult thing I did as council member was to site the new landfill. It was incredibly divisive. It's so exposed where the lines were, where the seams are in the city, with the rich on one side and everyone else on the other. It was very painful, but we did it.

Chester Jenkins was mayor around that time. Howard [Clement] was a council member for thirty years. Whether or not that's a good thing it depends on how engaged you are, how burned out you get, how excited you are about the possibilities and whether or not you're good at it. The way I look at it you have term limits every time you run. People look at you; they decide whether or not you should continue.

Durham Police

Seeing blue lights in the rearview mirror…the first thing that comes to my mind is "Oh, my God, what have I done wrong?" I've never gotten a ticket or been arrested. But I saw *Magnum Force* and *Straw Dogs* and a double feature when I lived in Charleston, and it stuck with me to this day. That has to be thirty-five years ago.

I used to live on Cherry Grove near Holton Middle School, and they used to do traffic stops there. The first time, I was terrified, and he said, "Well, ma'am, what's wrong?" And I said, "Oh, please don't kill me. Please don't kill me!" And he said, "Well, why would I kill you?" and I said, "Because you carry a Magnum and that's what you do!" This was like ten or fifteen years after that movie. He said, "Well, ma'am, I really just want to see your license and your insurance." This was right at Hyde Park and Main Street, and I had like less than a mile to go to my house and I drove shaking the rest the way home.

After I got on the council, I got to know some of the police, and they were really, really nice. Glendon Beard, Jackie McNeil, Officer Sarvis—he and his father and his son were all police officers. Sarvis…his beat was Few Gardens—the public housing complex where Edgemont Community Center was located. I was always having to call him in—there are drugs around, we'd been broken into, there was always something going on.

Of course when I was on the council I made sure that I was never ever doing anything that would be a problem [with the police]. Never drinking and driving—not anything. Not even a glass of wine.

So my relationship with the police has sort of matured, and now, as an older person, it's different. When I worked for DSS I parked in the handicap parking because I can't walk very fast or far. So I pulled to the spot and before I can put my placard up this officer pulls up beside me and is yelling at me. "You can't park here! It's a handicap space."

I told him I'm handicapped and showed him the placard. He said I should be displaying that. I explained that I was about to. Then I asked him why was he yelling at me, and he told me not to talk back to him. Fortunately, someone else came along, and that was the end of it. But let me tell you how long ago—that was it since they made Main Street two way. That's pretty recently. But in general my attitude has improved toward the police.

But now all of these killings have happened [recently], and I've become more aware of how the police interact with us although 1) I'm a woman, 2) I'm older and 3) they may not realize initially that I'm black and that none of those makes it okay, so my "spidey" senses are more heightened. I also recognize how uncomfortable it must be for good cops to be tarred with that same brush, to be trying to do their job, to be trying to go home to their families, to not be killed on the job. So I've been working through my thoughts about the police.

Working with DSS

The first time I was there, I worked in daycare services. That lasted six or eight months. Then I moved to adult services and loved, loved, loved it. I could really connect with them. In fact, my supervisor realized this and came to divert the most difficult cases to me. I wanted to get better at it and wanted to go to grad school, so I did. And when I went back [years later] as a trainer, I developed program orientations and so forth. I began supervising people—Medicaid and food stamp trainers. We went through some directors.

Then the last one came…and left, but not before she did some damage. And some of the damage that she did was to me. She didn't like me from the minute she met me. So one Thursday while she was in a meeting with Sharon Hirsch, my boss, she had Sharon come get me and bring me into the office. Sharon had this weird look on her face. The director said, "On Monday, you're going to start work in adult services. There'll be no change to your salary, and you need to pack all your things and move over there. Do you have any questions?"

I asked had I done something wrong? She said, "No, I'm just reorganizing." I said that I would need to tell my staff. She said, "No, don't worry—I'll tell them." [The director referenced here is Gerri Robinson, who was subsequently terminated by the county under allegations of discrimination against Caucasian staff members, including Sharon Hirsch.]

So I moved over to adult services. What she had neglected to mention was that this was a position that had been posted and the supervisor had done all of her interviews and was ready to make an offer. She [the director] didn't let the supervisor make an offer. She put me into the position. So I'm going into a new unit, working in the area of guardianship (where I had worked maybe twenty years before and it's all different now) and in-home services.

So on Monday, I present myself to this person, my new supervisor, say hello my name's Diane Wright and I'm told I'm supposed to report to you and she took me in and she taught me everything I needed to know. I had a caseload that went from New Bern to Pinehurst. And I had to see everybody every month. So, if you're adjudicated incompetent in Durham, they send you back to wherever you're from, but your case is managed from Durham.

A difficult setup, but I was phenomenal. I learned the job. I did good. I got it organized. I had to see each of those people every month and then my in-home services people I had to see I think every three months and had a talk to them every month. An amazing amount of paperwork.

Kathy, my new supervisor, was very different from any supervisor I'd had before. She was very stern, didn't have an overt sense of humor, but she knew her job and she was fair. I'll take fair. We found a way to work together.

When I left she gave me the most beautiful compliment. She said, "I know when you came here it couldn't have been easy [Wright pauses, crying], but you carried it with grace and I really appreciate that." I told her I knew my being there must've been very difficult for her and that I thought she carried it off beautifully.

I still see her. I call her on her birthday and I saw her on the street the other day, and she tooted her horn, called out to me, "Hey, you can come back to work any day!"

Do I miss it?…I don't miss doing that job. I would've loved that job when I first worked there, but I was too old for that job, but I managed to get it to where I could see twelve people in a day. I was efficient. My mother was very organized. We rode the bus everywhere; she would plan out everything we were going to do. And Daddy was a parcel postman and all of that just, clicked in. I'd reserve Mondays and Fridays for paperwork days.

What do we need to do as a society to bring ourselves together more?

I think a lot of what gets played out is mean-spirited. Whether it's police beatings or not wanting gay people to be married or church bombings or whatever. There's an element of fear. One of the things that I think has helped the gay movement is that gays themselves have allowed themselves to be out. My sister was gay. Never in my life could I imagine being hateful toward anyone else because they're gay. As more and more people realize they know someone who's gay—someone they already love, they already respect or already like enough to have a soda with—and they find out that person is gay then I think that kind of problem will go away. I think that's transferable to other situations in younger people don't seem to care so much.

There will always be problems. There will always be crazy people. The way "crazy" plays out varies a great deal. It can be very random. People need to have experiences—meaningful experiences—not just sitting next to each other on the bus [or in] church. Not that those are bad things that just not enough to really change people. They need to have dialogue; they need to work on a project. When you go on a military base, you don't see that kind of garbage. It's about the job.

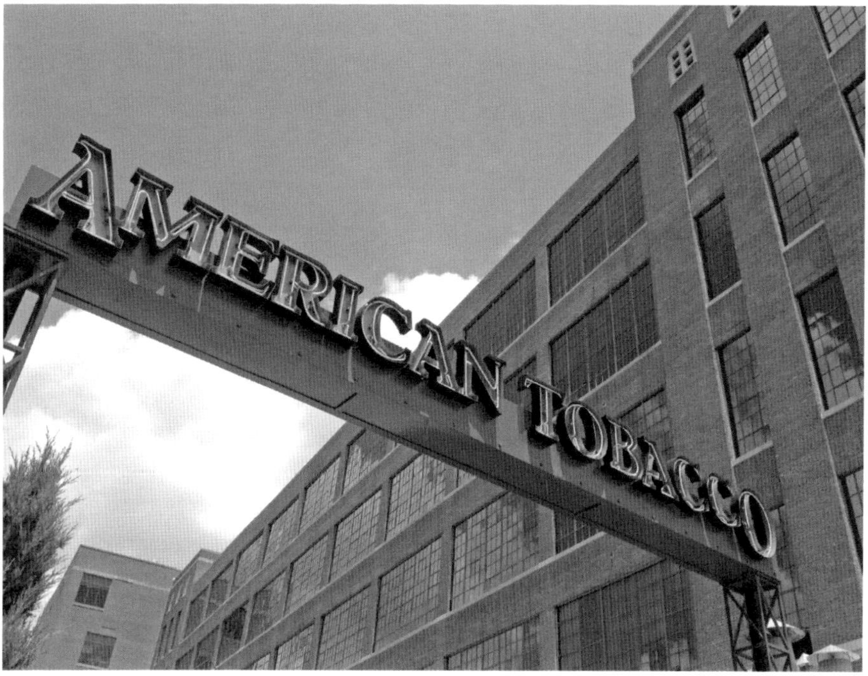

Durham today: The American Tobacco Campus entrance. *Photograph by the author.*

On the day of Diane's interview, July 7, Durham resident Lucille Ervin celebrated her 108th birthday. We talked about how people who live a long time and are happy and thriving (like Ervin) tend to be optimistic and able to deftly pivot away from the negative things that they witness and experience in life.

I think that our parents teach you "how to be" in the world. If I'd been a boy, they certainly would've given me the "little black boy talk" all of my male cousins got from their mothers. Mother used to say that we have to be twice as good as everybody else at whatever we try to do to even be accepted. You have to work twice as hard to get an A.

I've come to a rapprochement with my mother and some of her lessons. I think she felt that she had only a limited time to convey to me what she needed to because she was on like her third cancer when she died. She was drumming it in.

I knew that she had had thyroid cancer, two mastectomies and she died in 1964. I knew it was cancer; I knew it was bad. My mother was a nurse. I was relieved when she died both for her because she suffered greatly but also for me because in the end she was very, very mean to me.

Some of it was just about beating me bloody. Sister and I talked. She was like, "Mommy's not like that." It was like when an animal is wounded and will snap at you. I think [what] my sister thought was maybe that was just the part of Mommy that you got to see but I never saw that.

When my mother died, my sister was in Gary, Indiana. And after the funeral she moved to Germany and she never came back…because a black lesbian woman in the 1960s—there wasn't any place for her.

My parents never talked about her being gay, but they knew. My mother was always very loving and supportive toward her, and for that, I'm very grateful.

Mother didn't want us to learn to hate, so she didn't take me to the movies very often for me to have to go up into the balcony and climb all those stairs. When they integrated the movies, the first thing I ever saw was *Lolita* with my mother. My parents are very open-minded as far as books and reading material went. When we traveled, we drove—we didn't take buses and trains. When we would go to department stores, I got the talk before we left—don't touch anything, eat before you go. I never ate at a segregated lunch counter, never tried on clothes before buying them.

President Obama's Election

I was very pleased as I'm sure almost anybody who's black is going to answer. I've just been terrified all the time that something bad was going to happen him. I think Michelle Obama is just phenomenal.

8

MICHELLE JOHNSON

The first time I went to Kenya, I went to the Masai village, and it's the first time I really felt like I was home. It was like…I never felt this way before.

Born in Richmond, Virginia, Michelle Johnson moved to Chapel Hill in 1996 to come to school at UNC–Chapel Hill. Her mother was a special education teacher for over thirty years in inner-city Richmond. Michelle Johnson represents the new generation of African-American leadership. She's a social worker and a yoga instructor. She's an elected leader and the sole African-American voice on the board of aldermen.

In her politics, she is strong without being loud or strident. She's balanced. If you're familiar with the practice of yoga, you know that it requires a combination of strength and flexibility as well as a focused and centered mind. Johnson displays these traits in her yoga and her politics.

My dad…I didn't grow up with my dad…so that henceforth he lived in Arizona. He married my stepmother. His family is from Alaska, and he had a helicopter flight business and was in that business with her. I was two or three when it happened. Before that, he played football, and he had some other jobs Richmond. He played for the [Baltimore] Colts when they won the Super Bowl twice. He played for the Broncos and the Redskins for short amounts of time. He got injured and then ended up going to Hawaii to play in another league. His name is Cornelius Johnson.

I went to private school in Richmond. My mom was a public school teacher in inner-city schools, and she felt like we needed to go to private school.

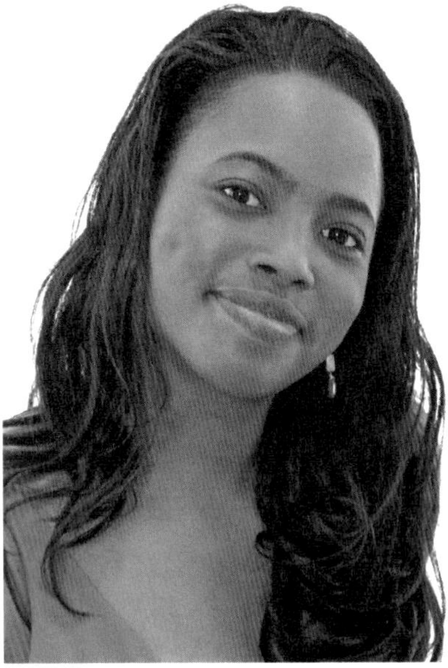

Michelle Johnson. *Photograph by Scott Chelmar; courtesy of Michelle Johnson.*

She didn't think that we [Michelle and her elder brother] would get a good education there [in public school].

She was conditioned to think that private school would be better for her kids of color. Better opportunity better education…she was conditioned that way. I'm not sure that's true but what that did was shelter us in many ways.

I was the only black girl in my class until ninth grade. There might've been others, but I do remember that. Then I went in tenth grade in an all-girl Catholic school (I'm not Catholic).

I think it was more of an issue in terms of socioeconomic status. We didn't have much money and I was on scholarship there and I would go home and say, "Mom, we're going on this trip and I want to go." She would say, "You're not like the other kids." She didn't let me know that it was because of that. She didn't say it was because of that, but I think by middle school, I could really tell.

I would go to my friends' homes and they would have domestic staff working at their house and my grandmother used to do that. So I kind of connected that—here's someone, this person who looks like me, cleaning the house, washing the dishes, doing things around the house while the parents are working or doing other things. I remember that that stood out to me, and I thought I never can have somebody else clean my house because my grandmother did that.

Some would treat their domestic staff very well—that was, they had a relationship. Others, not at all. Probably because their parents didn't model that. I never really talked to my friends about that, and it was very uncomfortable to be in that space because a lot of my friends had a lot of money. A lot of them had domestic workers in their home and, at that point, primarily black women.

I had a few friends who would come to my house. I had one friend named Allison Warner—we were best friends. I would go to her house, and when we would be at my house, we would do these things with potatoes. There's a way you can cut up a potato and then you can paint with it. Or we would bake cookies and when Allison would come to my house we would just have the best time. I felt like her parents never did anything with her that was fun or simple. She would love to come to my house because my mom would always have something for us, you know she was a teacher so she always had a fun activity. I had several friends that would come to my house. I'm not sure it was something that they would notice so much as their parents did, so I think it was more of an issue for their parents.

I was in high school when cotillions started. I was in a school that was white. All my friends were getting ready for cotillion. I wanted to do it; my mom didn't want me to. I stayed up all night crying. I insisted. She found a way. She made arrangements for me to go…and there I was that night the only black girl at cotillion. I've often thought about that how that was for her. I wanted to do it because my friends were doing it. My mom worked it out; she made my dresses.

I knew when I got there I was different. No white boy was gonna come up and asked me to dance. I'm different. I'm not like these other kids who were all around me. I'm in it like…I'm here.

Experience with Law Enforcement

"Moral Monday" protests were demonstrations held at the North Carolina general assembly to voice opposition to Republican-driven policies and budget cutbacks that were devastating to teachers and many vulnerable communities.

I was arrested for a Moral Monday protest. The charges were dropped, of course; after we returned to the next board of aldermen meeting, people stood up and clapped. It was great.

The town of Carrboro has been forward-leaning in seeking to improve the relationships between law enforcement and citizens. It's an area where elected leaders say they want constant improvement. To accomplish this, they have held public forums and anti-racism training sessions.

Carrboro police chief Walter Horton said at the first racism forum—we were talking about whether or not racism exists as if we could resolve that—and the chief said, "When I go to other communities I'm afraid." He's up there, he's a police chief, a man of color with a gun, and I thought, "What is this like?" He's a person with a lot of power, and that power is stripped away if he goes to another community and he's in the wrong place at the wrong time and he feels that. What an amazing admission to say that you have all this power and that it can be taken away. I felt that when he said that, that went deep.

Charleston

We talked about the visceral effects of overt racism and the shock to the senses brought on by the murders that had just occurred at the Mother Emanuel AME Church in Charleston, South Carolina.

I just went to the mountains, and I saw more Confederate flags (traveling by myself)…having panic attacks driving in the car looking at all these Confederate flags—more than I've ever seen. I've never been afraid like that, never felt like if I have a sheriff following me and I look like the wrong person to be in this neighborhood. I'm out here in the middle of nowhere; nobody knows where I am.

It's not all over. It's not socially acceptable. For me, it's being in a space that's not familiar to me and feeling like if my car breaks down on the side of the road—what's going to happen. I feel it. I feel it in my body. I mean I'm aware of racism, I am a "Dismantling Racism" trainer, but it's never felt this way.

I understand better why people get hypertension from the anxiety. I don't need to be driving down the road having a panic attack because of all these Confederate flags. Then there's the urge to go anyway. Am I making a statement or am I just driving down the road?

Maybe corporate America is more nuanced in some ways, but capitalism is at the core. They're not doing it driven by doing the right thing. They're doing it, driven by making money.

Graduate School at Carolina

William and Mary is small and UNC is huge. At William and Mary, I graduated in three years. I really didn't like it; I wanted to get out of there as soon as possible. I felt isolated there and I wanted to get out. When I came to Carolina, it was so huge…but my class at the school of social work … there were only thirty-seven of us. So they felt like family, and it seemed like all this is what college feels like for some people. For me, developmentally, it felt like college. William and Mary felt like middle school. I think it was the department I was in at UNC; we were social workers after all. That space felt really good. I remember the first couple of days of orientation we had a daylong diversity training and I thought this was really good that we're having this. I find that I'm in a lot of those conversations and I always wish that they'd be deeper but I was appreciative that they did it.

I lived in Chapel Hill and then I moved Carrboro. Now I do mainly social work but I integrate yoga into the therapy if my people want that. I actually talk about activism a lot when I teach yoga. I encourage people to think about something bigger.

TRAVEL

I've been to Kenya three times, and I'm going again at the end of July. I volunteer with the Africa yoga project. My partner, Jeff, and I are ambassadors for them. This year we're taking a group with us. We'll be building desks at a school and a community toilet. I've been to Paris and Ireland.

If I were going to live somewhere else in the world I think I would live in Kenya. My project is based in Nairobi, and it's very chaotic there. The first time I went to Kenya, I went to the Masai village, and it's the first time I really felt like I was home. It was like…I never felt this way before. I'm not sure if it's because people of East Africa look like me and like my mom does, but I just felt at home.

I want to do (genealogical research) now. I'm not scared of it. I know that my great-grandmother wasn't a slave, but her parents were. What I know of

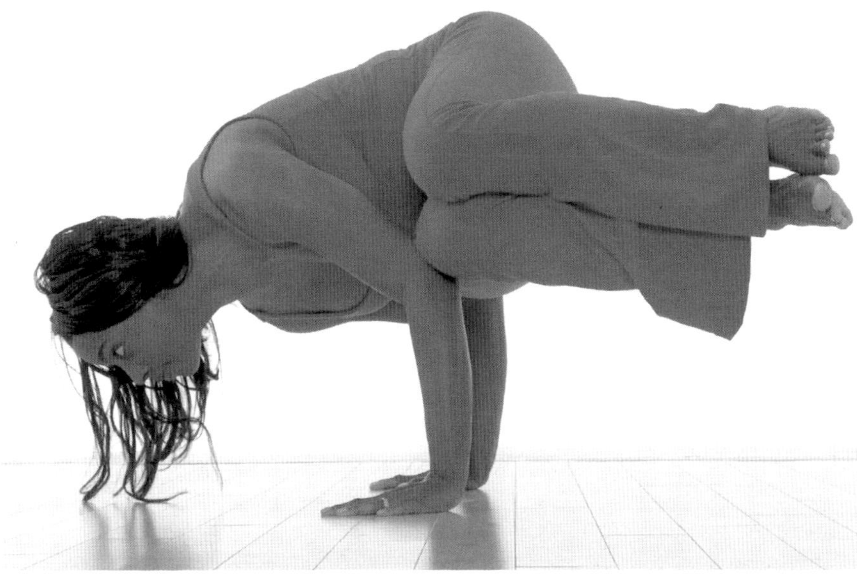

Michelle Johnson displays a new generation of strength and perspective. *Photograph by Scott Chelmar; courtesy of Michelle Johnson Yoga.*

the family history is already upsetting and traumatic, so it doesn't feel like what I find out would be worse than what I already know. And we don't know a lot because history wasn't passed on and people don't talk about it. My great-grandmother was senile when I came along. I wanted to know the stories, but she couldn't really tell me.

Because of cultural oppression or racism, we are trained to overlook parts of history and not look at the parts that we perceive as negative. We're very well trained in not looking at that. We talk in code sometimes. It could be easy for somebody to come to Carrboro and say, oh, it's great—there's Weaver Street Market, there is music on Sunday—and not really notice that there's not that many people of color hanging out on Weaver Street. Where they are, they tend to be the same people. It's at least not racially diverse. It doesn't feel that way to me.

There aren't that many folks of color. Numbers have dwindled over time. That's a socioeconomic issue, too. I remember I went canvassing with Ellie Kinnaird. She came with me and we would go to houses, and she would say these people are at risk for losing their house because of taxes. I just felt like…in ten years are there going to be any black folks in Carrboro? I mean probably people that work here, but I'm just thinking that…I'm not from Orange County so I don't want to talk out of turn, but I do feel like I'm not sure their history has been heard or celebrated. If folks already feel like they're not included or the system is not for them, but is designed to kill them or to keep them out in certain ways, then of course the message is my history is not important.

Carrboro Police Forums

I think that the community's building a relationship with police officers and I think the way that we're doing it is unusual. "Coffee with a Cop" has restarted and other initiatives, too. I think that while it's urgent, it takes time to build a relationship. So there are things like the way the room was set up last time, this kind of us-them arrangement, but I'm familiar with group dynamics and this is not unusual. We had two meetings, and you know it's only the second meeting. We can't expect this divide to be closed. People need to get to know each other, and they don't know each other.

This other alderperson and I were talking about sharing a meal or having a meal at the forum or something that is just not so set up to be adversarial. The police are set up to be in a position where they're defending their department.

And I think acknowledging that too would be good. It's going to take time, and it's about building relationships. Culturally I think the officers are not used to this, with engaging with the public in this way. The community's not used to it either, but I think wants it.

Maybe there are things that we will learn from these forums that other area police departments will learn from. We have a plan, and we're working through the plan.

ELECTION NIGHT 2008

I was at my friend's house. I think it was unbelievable. I didn't think in my lifetime I would see a black president; that was not something I thought to experience. It took a while for it to sink in. I was just crying. I interviewed my grandmother after that. She told me a lot of things that I would've thought would've made her emotional, but the thing that did make her emotional was talking about Barack Obama. She's ninety-four years old, and she thought this is never happening in her lifetime. I was with my grandmother and my mom in 2012 on election night and that was really neat to be with them. Then, of course, I've been really terrified that he would be assassinated—I mean really terrified. So I felt a lot of pride and I was excited, but then there's been this worry along with it.

Since the 2012 elections, he must just be worn out from the politics. I feel like the racism has always been present but I feel like there's been just a backlash from his election. The white supremacy that we're seeing now I think is directly connected to his election to the point where folks of color—when we're by ourselves—we feel like we can't wait 'til he gets out of there because we don't want another black person killed. That's the deal. It's just terrible to think that way.

I wonder how he feels about this. I want to know how his heart feels, how he is. It must be a burden. Being in this most powerful position and then seeing your people...you can't change white supremacy and racism, nor was that his charge or goal.

9

THE KLAN

Some stories we'll gladly remember.
Others, we should ensure we never forget.

Begrudgingly, it is necessary to finish these stories not on an uplifting note or suggestion that we will live happily ever after but instead on an expression of worry and sadness.

After the snakes in his dresser drawer that Floyd McKissick Sr. endured and the taunting that Brenda Stephens kept from her mother most of her life, there still exists the disease of white supremacy and its overt symptom—the Ku Klux Klan. There is still squabbling over the propriety of displaying a Confederate battle flag.

It has even leeched onto the 2016 presidential race.

In 1987, as photographer and filmmaker Michael Galinsky had just graduated from high school in Chapel Hill, there was a Klan march on Franklin Street. Galinsky ran across the images in the spring of 2015 and these nearly forgotten images made the local news. It was striking to many how long ago Klan marches seemed. It is a chapter of our story as a community whose end we eagerly anticipate.

In May 2015, he wrote about the experience on his blog at rumur.com in an entry called "The Day the KKK Came to Town."

I started taking pictures voraciously in high school, and took many of the pictures in the school newspaper and the yearbook. However, the day after graduation was the first time I photographed what could be called a news event.

I have no visceral memories from that day. I can't tell you what it felt like, and I can't really remember snapping the pictures. Perhaps this is one of the

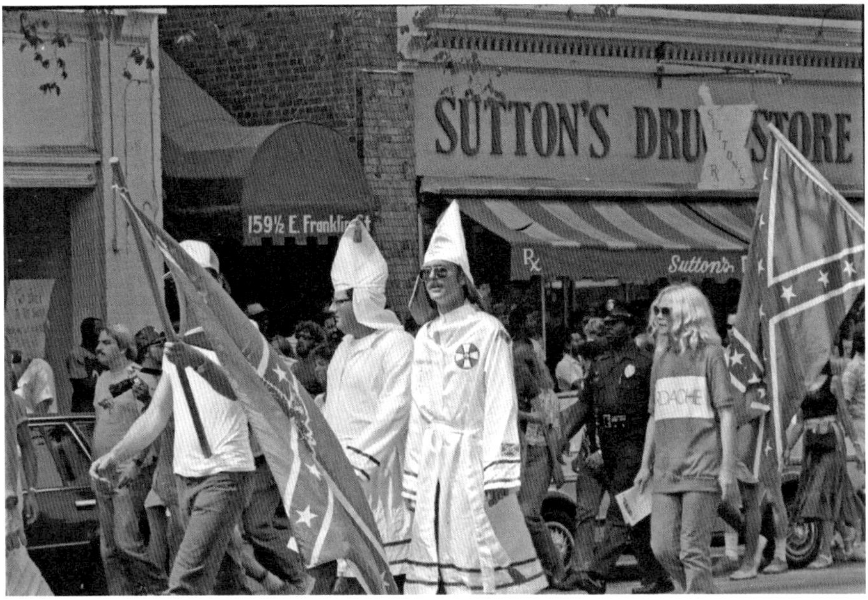

KKK march in Chapel Hill on June 14, 1987. *Photograph by Michael Galinsky.*

reasons that I have always been drawn to taking pictures. They stop time in ways that my brain is not so adept at doing.

Yesterday I found a couple of faded prints from that Klan march, and I posted them to Facebook. Then I stumbled onto the negatives in the same box, prompting me to fix my iPhone scanner and go through the images. The more I looked at them, the more I began to remember that day.

Just this afternoon, I realized that tomorrow is the sixtieth anniversary of *Brown v. Board of Education,* so I decided to post them to our blog.

I grew up in Chapel Hill, North Carolina, and went to public school shortly after desegregation. Despite the fact that my parents were Northeast transplants who were involved in civil rights issues, I wasn't acutely aware of race until I entered junior high school. At that point, there was a good deal of social separation, but I don't recall a great deal of direct racism. That is to say, I wasn't aware that the Klan even still existed until they decided to march in Chapel Hill the day after my high school graduation in 1987.

I found out it was the day after graduation by Googling the event, which led me to a *New York Times* article. Then another friend commented on my post to tell me that he had been angry that I went to the parade because many people felt that protesting the Klan was giving them the attention they desired. I imagine that I wanted to see it for myself, and I was excited to have something "real" to photograph.

The first time I connected to a memory that stirred up emotions from that day was when I found this image of a noose hanging from a mirror. I recall feeling shocked, and nervous. It felt dangerous enough that I stayed back and shot it with my telephoto lens. I felt as if I drew attention to it with my camera, that I would somehow be putting myself in danger.

I recall only a handful of Klan members, but the *Times* put the number near forty. I do know that many more than that came out to protest the event despite local religious leaders' request that the Klan be greeted by an empty street to walk down. Too many people wanted to fight back about this incursion of overt racism in the liberal bastion that Jesse Helms famously suggested they should put a fence around.

Having recently moved back to North Carolina from Brooklyn, New York, I have been a bit surprised to see how entrenched social segregation is in Chapel Hill. Our town is not alone. Many studies show that school segregation is increasing at a rapid pace. We can all look back and be proud of what we have achieved in terms of limiting overt discrimination. However, if we look around and see that there is a lot of work to be done to bring true equality and justice to our country, we can't sit around and expect others to do it for us. Let's let this day be a reminder that we still have a long way to go.

Since Michael was just graduating from high school that summer, I do not expect him to realize it, but that was not the "day the KKK came to town." It was just a day when they marched on Franklin Street. They did not come from somewhere else. They already live here.

As I left my role as chair of the brand-new Human Relations Commission (sometime in the early 1990s), I gave my last report to the Orange County commissioners. I reported the work we had done, the hearings we held on employment, housing and public accommodations discrimination. I reviewed the local civil rights ordinance we had created, but I cautioned them, too. "The Klan is alive and well in this county," I said.

A friend told me later that there were Klansmen—several of them—sitting in the rows right behind the microphone where I stood to address the commissioners. They did not glow in the dark. They were not waving a flag, but my friend, a lifelong Orange County resident, knew who they were. Alive and well.

That was twenty-five years ago.

As a community and a nation, we are in an important moment in race relations. We can actually start to see a way forward that is better. Much better. If my white brothers and sisters can continue learning and growing on the tender subject of white privilege and the

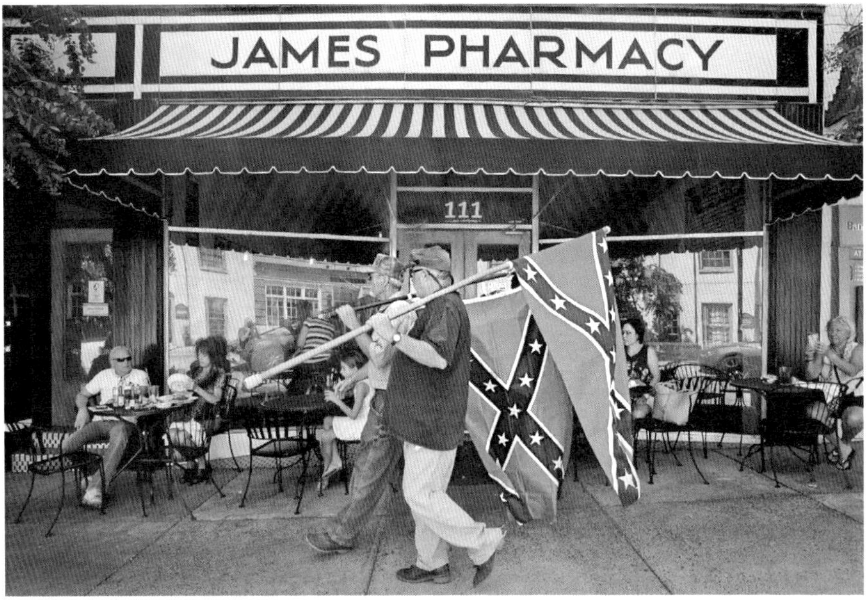

Unnamed demonstrators walk along Churton Street displaying their Confederate flags in Hillsborough, North Carolina, on August 8, 2015. The flag rally event was held in protest of the removal of the Confederate battle flag from the grounds of the South Carolina capitol in Columbia. *Photograph by Chuck Liddy; courtesy of the* News & Observer.

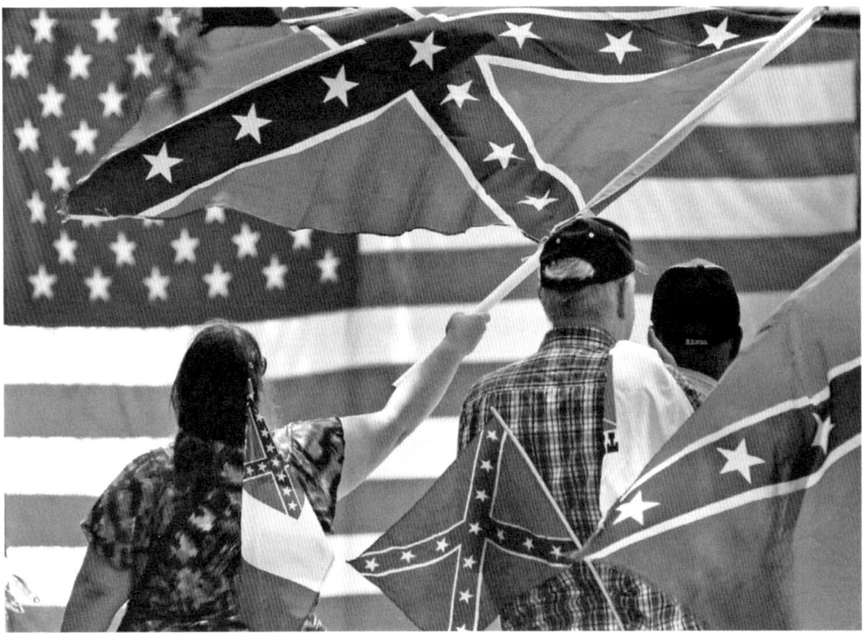

Flag wavers attend a Confederate flag rally in Hillsborough, North Carolina, on August 8, 2015. *Photograph by Chuck Liddy; courtesy of the* News & Observer.

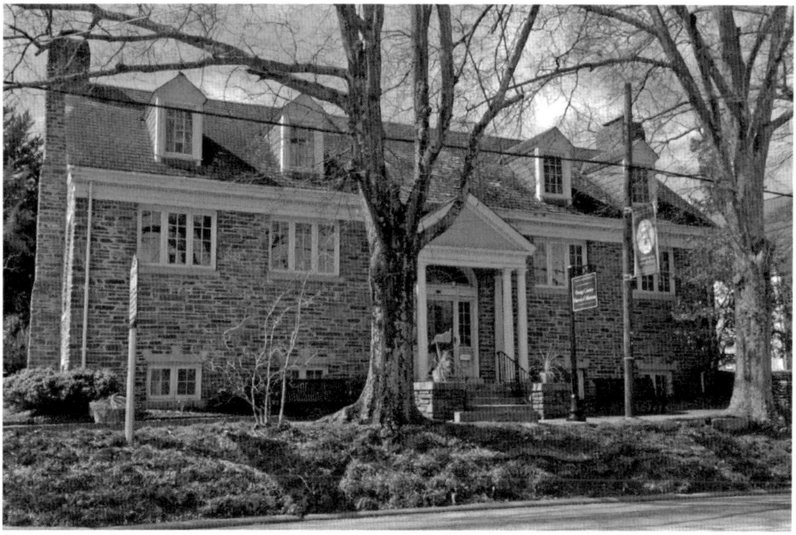

Orange County Historical Museum, 2016. Formerly the Confederate Memorial Public Library. *Photograph by the author.*

fact that we have it, have benefited from it and must dismantle it for our own sake, then we can move forward. There is resistance to this idea—a lot of it. Still, the tectonic changes are happening. You can feel the earth moving and hearts changing with it. Today, the Klan is still alive, but under withering attack, like the viral infection that it is.

The Klan is like the common cold—a viral infection. We never really get rid of the common cold. Our bodies' immune systems adjust and control the virus, but once you contract a cold virus, you have it as part of your body for the rest of your life. The United States and the South have carried the virus of racial bigotry throughout their history. Across the arc of history, we have treated symptoms, and we have gotten better. We are adapting. We are regaining our strength, and that hacking cough of nationalism and fearmongering may just be the last dose of expectorant we needed.

In 2015, there was a rally along Churton Street in Hillsborough celebrating the Confederate flag in the wake of the Charleston, South Carolina murders that resulted in the removal of the Confederate battle flag from the South Carolina state capitol grounds. Most of the folks attending the rally did come from out of town, and they displayed their flags without incident as the locals picnicked on the town common.

It was a comfortable summer day, damaged only slightly by the unwelcome and unrequested flags that flashed a sea of stars and bars and flaming red history.

Following the rally, the local debate ensued about the words "Confederate Memorial Library" remaining on the Churton Street building (now a museum). By year's end, those words were stricken from the building and rendered to history, where they belong.

Index

R

S

W

ABOUT THE AUTHOR

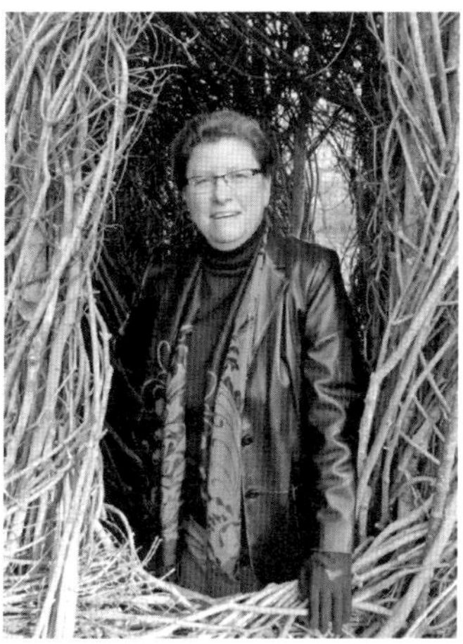

Jean Bolduc, author. *Photograph by Jamie Hagenberger.*

Jean Bolduc is a freelance writer who has lived in North Carolina since the late 1970s and in Chapel Hill for most of that time. She is a graduate of the University of North Carolina at Chapel Hill with a bachelor's degree in journalism and mass communication. She has worked for the *Herald-Sun* newspapers as a reporter and columnist and for the *News & Observer* as a reporter, covering local government. She was a nominee for the University of Oregon's Payne Award for Ethics in Journalism.

In between newspaper jobs, Jean has worked in the public sector as a public information officer and communications director for the Durham Housing Authority and as a private communications consultant working with clients in several states.

She and her husband, Rick, have two sons, Brian and Robert.